ONLINE BUSINESS

3 Manuscripts -Passive Income Ideas, Amazon FBA for Beginners, Affiliate Marketing

Mark Smith

PASSIVE INCOME IDEAS

*Proven Steps and Strategies
to Make Money While Sleeping*

Mark Smith

This document is geared towards providing exact and reliable information in regards to the topic and issue covered. The publication is sold on the idea that the publisher is not required to render accounting services, officially permitted or otherwise. If advice is necessary, legal or professional, a practiced individual in the profession should be ordered.

- From a Declaration of Principles which was accepted and approved equally by a Committee of the American Bar Association and a Committee of Publishers and Associations.

The information provided herein is stated to be truthful and consistent, in that any liability, in terms of inattention or otherwise, by any usage or abuse of any policies, processes, or directions contained within is the solitary and utter responsibility of the recipient reader. Under no circumstances will any legal responsibility or blame be held against the publisher for any reparation, damages, or monetary loss due to the information herein, either directly or indirectly.

The information herein is offered for informational purposes solely and is universal as so. The presentation of the information is without a contract or any type of guarantee assurance.

The trademarks that are used are without any consent, and the publication of the trademark is without permission or backing by the trademark owner. All trademarks and brands within this book are for clarifying purposes only and are the owned by the owners themselves, not affiliated with this document.

Table of Contents

Introduction

I want to thank you and congratulate you for purchasing the book, *"Passive Income: Proven Steps And Strategies to Make Money While Sleeping"*.

This book contains proven steps and strategies on how to earn some extra cash without having to depend on your day job. In an age where economies are crumbling and jobs are being lost, you need to find new ways to use your time to make that extra buck. The idea of earning a secondary income is the way to go, and you can now leverage the advanced technology available to make money online. Passive income is not the wave of the future – it is already sweeping across the globe right now.

The first thing this book will teach is what passive income actually is. There are a lot of people who tend to get the wrong idea about what passive income really means. Here the record will be set straight. As you read this book, you will find yourself being asked some truly pertinent yet revealing questions about your passive income strategy. Be honest and think deeply about each one of these questions. They could end up determining whether you achieve success or failure.

This book will also define exclusively new and radical ways to develop a real passive income. You will learn how to make money on the side and still keep your day job if you wish. There are some strategies that will allow you to make money so fast that you may even be tempted to quit your day job and enjoy your life anew, doing the things that you really love.

One thing that has to be clearly understood is that this is not a get rich quick scheme. If you are expecting some kind of content on how to con people out of their hard-earned money, then this book is not for you. The strategies outlined here are simple business ideas and principles that you can leverage to create a passive income stream. If you can take the information in this book and implement the strategies, there is no reason why you should not succeed.

Thanks again for purchasing this book, I hope you enjoy it!

Chapter 1: What Is Passive Income?

In order to maximize your use of passive income to attain financial freedom, you have to first accurately understand the concept itself.

Passive vs. Active Income

Passive income is simply revenue that you earn without actively working for it. It is not like a regular job where you have to show up every day, put in time and effort, and may even get fired from. With passive income, money keeps on flowing in even if you do not go to work.

It is very different from active income, where you have a contract to work for a client or employer, and failure to do so results in loss of income. Some people tend to confuse the term passive income by including some types of "off-the-books" contract work. Just because the work you are doing offers you some kind of flexibility does not mean it is part of your passive income. As long as you have to do the work yourself, it is classified as active income.

The key thing to understand is that passive income allows you to get paid even though you are not actively engaged in doing any meaningful work. You may have to spend some time initially setting the business up and getting it off the ground, but there will come a time when you will be able to sit back and enjoy your passive income stream. You will actually have a choice of whether to continue working or not. An active income does not present you with this kind of freedom.

What Passive Income Is Not

There are some income streams that you may benefit from yet they cannot be truly categorized as passive income. A good example of this is receiving an inheritance or selling an asset. These are simply one-off lump sum payments that have no continuation over time.

Passive income is not necessarily risk-free. It cannot be defined as being totally secure income. Yes, there are some income streams that have less risk than others, but the truth is that every source of income carries some risk. Even with passive income, it is always wise to create multiple income streams in order to minimize the risk of failure.

Another thing that passive income is not is "maintenance-free."

At some point in time, you will have to step in to carry out some kind of maintenance to keep the income stream flowing steadily. It is a myth to believe that once you establish your source of passive income and step back, you no longer have to keep an eye on things. There are taxes to be filed, checks to be deposited, and even mail to be responded to. It may be small things here and there but they still need to be done.

When looking at the level of maintenance required in sustaining passive income, you need to determine whether it is very passive or semi-passive. A good example is writing a book versus renting out your house. With a very passive income like book royalties, you dot really have to do much once the book is published. The book will be sold in stores or online by the publisher and you will not be required to deal with customers. All you will have to do is cash in the royalty checks. With a semi-passive income like house rentals, you will be required to maintain the house on a regular basis. You may also have to look for new tenants, make insurance payments and taxes, and even supervise the building caretaker.

Finally, passive income is not a get-rich-quick scheme. If you have the idea that you can create a passive income stream by cheating people off of their hard-earned cash, then this book is definitely not for you. This kind of mindset should not be used to define a passive income. There are people who try to look for ways to make money without necessarily providing anything of value in return. This is not entrepreneurship – it is plain thievery.

It is true that there are loopholes in the economy that you can leverage to make some money for yourself. However, this type of approach should never be described as a passive income. You should always try to create value for your customers so that they are always willing and ready to give you their money. There are some businesses that require you to provide more value than others, but at the end of the day, you need to offer something to get money in return.

Key Questions To Ask yourself
Where will passive income streams lead me?

A lot of people jump into developing multiple income streams without clearly defining what their end game will be. You need to ask yourself how your life will respond to the successes you will achieve. How will that extra $1000 change your life? At what point will you be able to live off of your passive income? How will you spend your spare time once you start earning money passively?

Is passive income a recipe for success or failure in my life?

Would you invest your extra time and money on productive things in your life or would you laze around, get fat, do drugs, and ultimately die early? These are pertinent questions you cannot afford to skip. You need to decide how you will grow your life and share the value you have created with others around you. Otherwise, you will simply be tempted to engage in things that will bring you down faster than you came up. Many people have burned out or become depressed because they did not plan in advance how they would structure their new life.

Why do I need passive income streams?

What motivations do you have for creating passive income? Is it simply because you are constantly broke or in debt? You need to realize that your motivation for wanting that extra money is what will determine what your life looks like after you get it. The truth is that in most cases, you can still be happy with the little money you have, so ensure that your motivation is linked to attaining fulfillment and contentment.

Avoiding the Hype

There are many books and web articles out there that claim to teach you how to make a lot of money quickly. They may even say that their system is guaranteed to give you a passive income stream for free. You need to be careful with such schemes. A lot of innocent people have been swindled and lost money by falling for such strategies.

This book is not about creating money from thin air. There is something that will always be required of you when creating a passive income stream. These include time, energy, money, and commitment. Passive income always involves work, so do not get the wrong idea because you are desperate to pay your rent by next week. Making passive income work for you will require that you get down and dirty in the initial stages and make sacrifices just like every truly successful businessperson. There are no shortcuts in this book. Do the work first, and then start thinking about enjoying the results. Now let us take a look at some of the ways in which you can create a passive income that will transform your life, and take you one step closer to financial freedom!

Chapter 2: Invest In Real Estate

When you decide to venture into real estate investing to generate passive income, you have to consider what kind of approach to use. There are different strategies that you can leverage in order to find an approach that suits not just your financial needs but also your startup capital investment.

Turnkey Real Estate

A really good way to start generating passive income in real estate is through turnkey rental properties. Turnkey properties can be a golden opportunity for anyone who wants to start investing in real estate. So what are turnkey properties and why are they so special?

Turnkey real estate properties are simply properties that have already been renovated, usually by a property management company, and are on sale. You purchase the property from the real estate management company and rent it out, earning yourself a tidy sum every month. What makes this type of real estate investment popular is that the same company that managed the property before can provide you with management services after the sale. They will collect your rent, pay for maintenance and repairs, handle all the documentation, and send you your money. You do not have to deal with the renters yourself, so this saves you time and effort.

However, there are certain things that you have to consider as an investor before choosing this sort of passing income vehicle:

Research the Property

You have to know your property well before deciding to buy it. This means that you need to conduct proper research to determine whether the house is worth buying. You need to ask yourself if the value of the home is really what the seller is describing. A lot of rookie investors jump at the chance to buy a turnkey property only to realize that the property wasn't worth it.

The best way to know your property is to visit it in person and check it out. If the property is in another part of the country, you may have to send someone you trust to take a look at it, or even travel there yourself. Buying real estate is a massive investment that you cannot take lightly, and you need to make sure that what you get is of the same value as the money you are putting down. Visit the area and get a feel of how the place will develop in the future. Will the property still retain or increase its value considering the current trends in the neighborhood, or will its value drop?

You should consider what your cash flow will look like once you buy the property and rent it out. Choosing a property in a poorly kept neighborhood just because expenses will be low and income high is a bad idea. A high return always carries a high risk. You will be better off going for property that is in a well-kept area with good social amenities, even though monthly profits may be lower. Your property is more likely to appreciate in value with time.

It is also a good idea to involve a professional property inspector so that they can examine the details that most property management companies will not willingly reveal to you. You may be impressed by the finishing and renovations on the home, but what about the roof, HVAC system, or the plumbing behind the walls? A professional home inspector will be able to note down things that you may not see.

Get to know the character of tenants in the neighborhood

As a potential landlord, you do not want to have tenants who give you a headache every day. You need to visit the neighborhood to know the kind of tenants that live in the area. Tenants who are stable and responsible will be more reliable when it comes to paying rent on time. Some areas have tenants who break or damage property and move out without giving any notice.

Research the Vacancy Rates

Always make sure that you know the vacancy rate of the property you are investing in. A home or apartment with a high vacancy rate will not bring in a lot of money. It may be of high value or have the potential to appreciate in the future, but you also need to think about your property expenses. You are better off buying property that is able to bring in tenants on a regular basis.

Research the Property Management Company

There needs to be a lot of trust between you and the property management company. If you are going to work with them, then you need to have faith that they are experienced professionals who can be trusted to handle your issues. There is nothing as bad as dealing with a management firm that doesn't carry out repairs when they need to, or isn't diligent enough to look for new tenants. It is critical that you do a background check to determine certain aspects of the way the firm operates, such as:

- The fees that they charge

- Whether they provide monthly statements to help you monitor the income and expenditure on the property

- The time it takes them, on average, to fill rental property vacancies

- The years of experience they have

This information can be obtained by sitting down and talking to the property manager, but it would help you more if you talked to other clients who have worked with the firm.

Understand the Type of Agreement

You need to know what kind of ownership agreement you are getting into with the management firm. It could be that they want their name to stay on the title, so instead of selling you the property, they opt to become your partner through an LLC. It is in your best interests to buy the property outright to prevent future problems, so the recommended solution, in this case, would be to create an independent expense account to be used for maintenance purposes when necessary.

Understand the Potential Risks

Investing in real estate may be lucrative, but it definitely isn't for everyone. You should always be prepared for any risks or problems that may arise, for example, unforeseen property tax hikes. You need to have some money on hand just in case something unforeseen happens. Most people who choose to invest in real estate tend to do so for the long-term. There are always ups and downs in the property market, and it is best to be patient when investing in this sector. If you cannot do so, then you need not bother putting your money in real estate.

Making Money Through Airbnb

Airbnb is a peer-to-peer service that allows you to rent out your house or apartment for a short period of time. It is a great way to make some extra cash especially when you have room in your house that isn't being used. You may also be planning to go out of town for a while yet the rent still has to be paid, so why not rent out your apartment for the duration?

The Airbnb app allows you to list your property – which can be anything from a single room to a houseboat – on the Airbnb website for free. You can then promote your property by creating a profile with titles, descriptions, and photos. This information then helps guests to find a suitable place to stay in case they are in the area. Airbnb helps you connect to other people in the area who are looking for temporary housing.

A guest may go through the database by filling in details of where they are traveling to and when they will be in the area. How attractive or interesting your property will be to guests may depend on the type of room/space on offer, your rental price, the size of the space available, any amenities you may be providing, or even the language that you speak.

So how do you go about setting up a business using Airbnb?

Listing your Space

You are the one who decides when to rent out your space and the price to charge as rent. The listing process is free, and you can choose whom to rent to by approving potential tenants in advance. You will have to keep in mind that there are other people who may be renting out their spaces, so keep your price competitive.

You need to look at the costs of hosting a guest, for example, cleaning, utility bills, Airbnb's host charges, and taxes. If you intend to use the Airbnb service, you will need to comply with their hosting standards and regulations. These include how to list your property accurately, how to communicate with your tenants, maintaining your reservation obligations, hygiene standards, and provision of basic amenities like toilet paper and soap.

Your listing on the Airbnb website will include a photo of the room or house, so make sure that it is neat and presentable. You can take the picture yourself and upload it, or Airbnb may send a professional to take photos free of charge, though this is only for active hosts. You can even cross-promote your space on social media or via your personal website.

The way you describe your space will determine the level of interest it generates on the platform. Describe it in a unique way and from the perspective of someone who is not a local. This means that you should emphasize the nearest transit means available, the nearest entertainment spots and restaurants, and what the culture is like in the area. You should also elaborate on any additional benefits a guest may benefit from, such as cable TV, Wi-Fi, a fully stocked fridge, etc.

Getting Authorization and Paying Taxes

If you are renting an apartment or house and want to take in a paying guest, then you will have to get permission from your own landlord. In case your property is part of a co-op or homeowners' association, then you need to make sure that there is nothing in their rules that disallows hosting a paying guest. Airbnb always recommends that you add a rider to any contract you sign with the above entities to specifically deal with hosting via Airbnb.

There are also local income taxes to think about. The local authority may consider anybody renting out his or her space using Airbnb to be running a hotel, so there could be a transient occupancy tax to pay. You will also have to pay federal taxes.

Personal Security

If you are renting out a room in your apartment or house, you should carefully consider your personal safety. In case you are going on a trip, then you will have the headache of locking away anything of high value, just in case your guest has itchy fingers. It is recommended that you find out more about your tenant by looking at reviews written about them by previous hosts. You may also do some basic Internet detective work, or run a criminal background check (if you realistically can).

Payment Guarantees

Payment is done via Airbnb, and your money is released to you within 24 hours of the arrival of your guest. If there is something that the guest isn't happy with, they are allowed to report it to Airbnb within 24 hours to get a refund. Trying to get paid outside the Airbnb system is a bad idea as the guest can easily dupe you. In the event that you are caught receiving payments outside the platform, Airbnb reserves the right to stop doing business with you.

Creating a passive income stream via Airbnb is a great way for you to meet different and interesting people while making some extra money. You can easily rent out one of your spare rooms in your house for a short period of time, thus helping you to pay the bills or have some residual income. Investing in real estate via Airbnb maximizes the use of your real estate property as the rent will still be paid even when you aren't around.

Chapter 3: Create a Website and Start Blogging

There are a lot of people who have tried to make money online by setting up a website – and failed miserably. Then there are others who have been so successful doing it that they quit their day jobs and became passive income earners. What was the difference? The first group just didn't do it the right way.

Is it possible to make serious money by starting a blog, and if so, how do you do it? The truth is that you can definitely make a lot of money through creating a website and blogging. The secret is to use the right strategies and find the best way to monetize your efforts.

A great blog is all about content. If you have great content, people will keep coming back to your site and you will be able to make more money. A lot of people spend too much time trying to fool the Google search bots to popularize their site, but this approach is doomed to fail in the long-term. These are the guys who go around saying blogging can't generate passive income.

But the successful ones know how to do it the right way. You can either have a website that sells products or dispenses information. Whichever option you choose, go for something that you are passionate about and keep tweaking your strategy until you get it right. As long as you focus on producing content that your readers find valuable, you will be able to draw in more people and make tons of money.

So what are some of the strategies that you can use when trying to make passive income through blogging?

Contextual Pay Per Click Advertising

With Pay Per Click (PPC) advertising, you can use either Google AdSense or Yahoo Publisher Network (YPN).

Google AdSense is more popular because they will only show ads that are relevant to the niche that your blog caters for. It is also the easiest option to put in place.

YPN is a major competitor to AdSense. YPN, however, does not display ads that are as relevant to your content as Google does, so this might not appeal to your site visitors. On the other hand, YPN pays you more per click than AdSense, so it becomes a question of balancing short-term goals with long-term passive income.

If you are unsure of which one to pick, just start with the simplest option, AdSense, and test it out. Place the ads in different places on your site and move them around regularly. Monitor how effective the placement is. You can also change the color of the text or link to see how visitors respond to these alterations. Do not make multiple changes at the same time because if traffic skyrockets, there will be no way of knowing which change caused the upsurge. After a couple of months, you can change to YPN and track the changes in traffic levels. Testing different techniques and strategies is a great way to figure out what works best for your site.

Affiliate Marketing

The most successful Internet marketers use this strategy. A lot of people have tried to use this strategy, but the problem is that they used wrong techniques, failed to put in enough effort, and gave up midway. Picking the right system to use can keep you rolling in dough for a really long time.

The first step is to know your niche thoroughly. If your blog is about fitness, make sure you become an expert at it. The content that you place on your blog needs to be of high quality and authoritative. Readers can smell BS by simply reading your content and examining the facts presented.

Once you do this, it's time to find great products to promote.

Not just any products, but the ones that are selling really well. The simplest affiliate program out there is ClickBank. You sign up and then search for any products that your blog can promote via keywords, and receive a code that allows you to promote that product. There is also Commission Junction, which actually gives you better insights to the number of clicks you have sent, though the products on offer are not as hot as those on ClickBank.

Monetize by Displaying Ads

There are some bloggers out there who seem to have a problem with this strategy because they think placing ads on your site cheapens the content. The question you need to ask yourself is this – Are you willing to provide people with free and high-quality content and not get paid for it? You are reading this book because you want out of the regular 9 to 5 rat race. If you can get paid for writing about stuff that you actually enjoy, why not do it?

You need to start by producing great content for your readers, the kind of content that people find helpful and useful to their lives. Most visitors expect successful sites to have some ads, and the fact that you do not have any ads may make them think that you are not popular or authoritative enough. You do not have to charge visitors subscription fees or sell them anything. Ads can make you a lot of money while making your site seem credible.

So what is the best time to place ads on your blog? Should you wait until traffic reaches a certain number of visitors per day, or just dive right in? You need to look at it this way: If you wait until you have a specific number of hits per day, then that day may never come. The best strategy is to do it immediately. Why? The reason is simple. The moment you monetize your website and place ads on it is the moment you will get serious about producing great content to drive traffic. If you have a day job then it's highly likely that you won't have the time or energy to blog consistently. This will affect your traffic numbers. Placing ads from the get-go motivates you to start taking things seriously because there is money involved now.

Where you place your ads on your blog is not very important. You just have to tweak things regularly to find the best fit. Just make sure that the kinds of ads you allow on your blog are relevant to your content. The ads have to be useful and valuable to your visitors. Lack of relevancy will annoy and drive visitors away, and you will not make any money.

The best way to draw in advertisers to buy space on your blog is to create a page on your site that clearly explains how they can do so. In case an advertiser comes across your site, they can easily know your rates, the spots on offer, and how to buy your ad space.

Paid Text Link Adverts

This is a system where you sign up, search for link ads to place on your site, and get paid every time someone buys a link from your site. There are a lot of websites that use this strategy to generate revenue. You literally get paid to place links on your website.

The procedure is simple: Go to www.text-link-ads.com, sign up with them, fill in a form, and receive a tiny code snippet that you will then place in your blog. The name of your blog is then added to their marketplace. Whenever someone goes to the marketplace to buy links and decides to purchase them from your site, you receive an email. You then have to log into the Text-link-Ads marketplace to approve the ad. You will then get paid 50% of the revenue earned and the other 50% goes to text-link-ads.com as a fee. The key here is to set a good price for links on your blog. Make sure that you value your blog properly by comparing it to others in the same niche.

Sponsored Reviews

As a blogger, you can actually get paid to write reviews about products or services related to your content niche. If you are able to develop strong credibility with your readers, they will be more likely to believe you when you review a product or service. When a product seller or service provider sees just how credible you are and the large following you have, they will pay you to write a positive review of whatever they are trying to sell. Your readers might then be interested in finding out more about the product or service, and this generates potential sales for the seller.

There are a number of sponsored review marketplaces that you can sign up to, such as ReviewMe. This sponsored review website (www.reviewme.com) allows you to sign up, fill out a form, and they then add you to their marketplace. In case someone wants you to review his or her product, you receive a notification and can then negotiate a fee in exchange for a sponsored review.

Amazon Affiliate Program

This is a very popular affiliate program for Internet marketers. It is really easy to set up and you can start making money right away. You can place Amazon affiliate links on your site every time you write about a product that is being sold on Amazon.com. Everybody is familiar with Amazon as a great place to buy products, so referring people to the website will get you paid. The only issue with this strategy is that Amazon is very stingy with their fees. You only get paid 5% of the revenue that is generated via your blog. No other website pays this low.

However, it is still worth signing up. Sooner or later you will find yourself mentioning or reviewing a product that can be bought at Amazon. Placing a quick link to the product page on Amazon will help your readers gather more information while earning you a small sum at the same time.

Chapter 4: Create Online Video Tutorials

If you have a particular process or concept that you are really good at, and own a blog with relevant content, you may want to consider teaching it to people through a video tutorial. Leveraging the power of online videos is one of the best ways to get the word out about your skills in a particular niche. Videos tend to attract huge followings these days, and creating an online video tutorial can be a great way to earn passive income.

Creating a good quality video tutorial is not that complicated. If you know your niche well, adopt the right strategy, and use the right tools, you will quickly be viewed as an expert and develop a large online following. Before you begin making a video tutorial to earn some money, there are a number of factors that you have to consider.

Factors to Consider

Target Audience

This is one of the most important factors to consider before creating any kind of content. If you take the time to ask yourself who your target audience is, you will have a great chance to produce content that is valuable and useful. You need to look at the kind of content that you want to share and ask yourself what type of audience would appreciate it the most. Get to understand your target audience, what they like, how they think, and what kind of format will suit them best.

Your Target's Goals

Once you understand who your target audience is, you should know the goals that they intend to accomplish. Are their goals in line with the content you want to provide? Will your tutorial help them move closer to their goals? If their goals become part of your goals, you will undoubtedly be in a better position to help them.

Resources and Tools Your Audience Need

People will be attracted to your online content because you offer them resources and tools they need. That is part of creating value for your customers, as these resources and tools can help them achieve whatever goals they have. For example, if your audience is interested in learning how to assemble a home solar power kit, they are going to need a list of equipment to purchase, where to buy them, the prices, and safe assembly instructions. Your objective should then be how to help them acquire such information as easily as possible. Your video tutorials should be tailored towards bridging the gap between them and the resources they need.

Potential Affiliate Partners

The main aim of creating a video is to make money. This means that you will have to promote a product or service to your audience in exchange for cash. That is where affiliate programs come in. You should sign up for an affiliate program with companies that offer such partnerships so that you promote their products on the video and they pay you in return. It is important to note that having a decent-sized online following will help you negotiate how much you earn, and even open up doors to companies that do not have affiliate programs in place.

How to Plan your Process

You cannot dive right into making a video tutorial without having some sort of plan. This is where you sit down with pen and paper and think about what you are trying to accomplish using the video. How do you do this?

Know your Subject Matter

You must have complete in-depth knowledge of your subject matter. If you aren't yet well versed in that area, do your due diligence and get up to speed with what you need to know. A half-baked teacher will never be able to convince students that they know what they are talking about. Visit other blogs and forums relevant to your niche and look at the questions people frequently ask. Ask yourself what kind of problems or challenges your target audience tends to face and read up on that.

Prepare a Script

It is always a good idea to sound natural on video, but having a bullet-point script as a guide is critical in keeping you on point and reminding you of the next topic to be covered. You do not want to start figuring things out in the middle of a tutorial video. Proper planning will always help you create something unique and valuable.

Choose the Type of Video

You can decide to record your computer screen and guide the audience on how to perform specific actions. For example, you can show them how to sign up for an affiliate marketing program on a website. If you are using a screen recording, then you must make sure that the desktop background is clean. The computer display should not show any of your personal information or irrelevant programs running in the background. For screen casting options, you should consider high-quality programs like VirtualDub, Camtasia, ScreenFlow, or Camstudio.

Your video tutorial may incorporate you standing in front of the camera. If this is your mode of choice, you will need a DSLR, camcorder, or simply use your Smartphone.

You can also make video recordings using a slide show presentation. This is a great way to teach your audience as long as you can create your slides well. You can use software like Google Slides, MS PowerPoint or Keynote.

Your final option in choosing your video format is to combine two or more of the above formats.

Prepare your Audio

You can choose to record your audio via your computer's microphone, though the quality may not be that good. A good quality USB microphone may come in handy, and you don't have to go for an expensive one at all. An Audiotechnica microphone will only set you back $30.

A great acoustic environment means no loud gadgets humming in the background. Make sure that the surfaces do not reverberate sound and create an echo. If you want to have some interesting background music, you can go to any creative commons sites (for example ccmixter.org) that offer free licensed music. Make sure that your background music does not drown out or interfere with your voiceover.

Create your Affiliate Program Link

You can use the Pretty Link Plug-in on Wordpress to create a link that will enable you to make money from your video. This is the link that your audience will click on to go ahead and purchase any of the products or services you may have promoted in the video.

How to Create the Video

Once the planning process is complete, you can go ahead and record, edit, and export your video.

Recording your video tutorial should be easy now that you are familiar with the software and the format to be used. Just press the "Record" button and talk to your audience. Try to be friendly and create a personal connection with your audience. Just don't go overboard with theatrics as you may frustrate some of your serious viewers.

When it comes to editing your video, you need to use good software, some of which are paid while others are free. You can use ScreenFlow, iMovie, Adobe Premiere, or Final Cut Express. With great editing techniques, you can offer more value to your audience. You can highlight the important features, add text to ensure the smooth and clear flow of information, or even remove mistakes in the video recording. A well-edited video will always transition well and stick to the point. Any unnecessary pauses, delays in loading, or slip-ups in speech should be cut out. In case you cannot edit the video yourself, you should consider outsourcing the work to a professional.

Exporting your video simply means converting it from the editing format into a format that can be easily uploaded onto your video streaming platform (YouTube, Udemy, etc.).

How to Publish the Video

When it comes to choosing which video streaming service to use for your online content, you can never go wrong with YouTube. Remember, you want to make money from your video, so you need to use a platform that is the second largest search engine on the web. The traffic that goes through YouTube every day is insanely huge, and you have the opportunity to tap into it for free. You can also post the video tutorial on Udemy or your own business blog.

How to Optimize the Video

The title of your video is the most critical part of the video, for obvious reasons. You want to be found easily on the Internet, so make sure that you use SEO and relevant keyword in your title and description. Make sure that people and the search engines will know exactly what your video contains. Don't forget to place a link to your website within the description area to enable people to visit your site. You should also write a blog post based on the same topic and embed the video into it.

How to Promote your Video Tutorial

There are various ways to promote your video tutorial. You can:

- Send it to your email list
- Promote it on the sidebar or navigation bar of your blog
- Share it on social media
- Share it with other bloggers who have a similar audience
- Share it with companies whose products you can promote

Videos are a great way to reach millions of people worldwide. Viral videos are making a huge impact on people, so you can never go wrong with making a video tutorial.

Chapter 5: Sell Digital Informational Products

The Internet has totally revolutionized the way people buy and sell products. This has had the effect of opening up the world to everyone who has something valuable to offer, whether it's a product or a service.

When it comes to earning a passive income online, one of the best things to do is to sell a digital product. With just a little effort put in, you can be able to create an informational product and sell it at an affordable price. Think of all the products on sites like Amazon, Etsy, or EBay. The digital products on these online selling platforms are very cheap and the demand keeps soaring year after year. If you can create an awesome informational product and sell it online, you can earn money for years.

What is an Informational Product?

An informational product is simply a product that is created to provide more information or knowledge about a specific topic or theme. Think of things like eBooks or videos that teach you how to do something. An informational product gives you the opportunity to create value for your customers in a quick and easy way.

There are two fundamental reasons why creating and selling an informational product is a great idea:

- It enables you to make passive income without having to invest too much time. Think of it this way. Once you finish creating that "How-To" eBook or video, you simply sell it on a digital platform like Amazon.com or your own website, and move on to other things. Better yet, if you are offering some kind of service through a website, you can create an informational product to accompany your services, and thus add value to your existing business. Informational products tend to sell themselves. That's the beauty of online platforms. You can even take a break from running your business and still be comfortable knowing that your digital informational product is out there selling itself and making money.

- A digital informational product allows you to reach potential clients who are on a low budget or aren't sure whether to work with you or not. By referring them to your informational product, you can allow them to use your know-how at an affordable price, and thus build trust over time. Once they know that you have the expertise in a certain area and trust you, they are more likely to come back to purchase more products or services from you. Furthermore, they are also likely to refer you to other clients. An informational product can be shared with others and easily generate positive reviews for you. You have suddenly locked in current and future clients.

Factors to Consider before Creating an Informational Product

When deciding on what kind of informational product to create, you will have to look at your personal interests, business interests, the amount of time you have, and the needs of your target customers. Creating a passive income may be a great way to earn money easily over the long-term, but it still involves a lot of work in the initial stages.

You will have to take into account things like the length of time the product will take to create, the initial financial investment required, and the amount of money you would like to make in profits per hour.

There's an old saying that says, "You write what you know."

When deciding what to write about or create a video about, the best bet you can make is to create a product that you are knowledgeable about. At this point, there are two things to think about:

- Commonly asked questions

In whatever business or line of work you are engaged in, there are certain questions that clients constantly ask. You can talk to customers about their concerns, or visit the FAQ page of a relevant website in the niche you want to tackle. Instead of answering questions via long emails, you can cash in by writing an eBook or creating an online video explaining everything that clients need to know.

- Basic services that you can provide

There are probably certain basic services that you perform day in day out. If you have a website and find yourself outgrowing certain services, you can create videos of how to perform those services for your clients. If a client with a small budget comes and wants to hire you to do something for them, you can simply ask them to purchase and download the video. It will be cheaper for the customer and allows you time to engage in other activities.

Creating Your Informational Content
Writing an eBook

The great thing about selling an eBook is that you do not have to be a writer to do it. If you are an SEO expert, you can get a freelance ghostwriter to write the book for you. The same applies to you if you are a designer or software developer. It doesn't matter what your expertise is. If you can put your knowledge in written format that can be digitized and monetized, you will always find someone willing to buy it. EBooks are pretty hot right now, and you can never go wrong with them.

Making Audio and Video Content

You can make podcasts or videos where you give people information that is not easily found. You do not have to be an expert, because no matter how little you know, there is always someone else who knows less than you. If the price is right, customers will choose to buy from you.

Creating an Online Community or Forum

If you have a lot of information that you are willing to share with an exclusive group of people, you can create a members only pay-for-admittance forum. The website should have a constant flow of relevant and high-quality information that people would be willing to pay good money for. If you are a guru in start-ups, SEO, stock trading, etc., you can charge your members to gain access to top-notch information that cannot be found elsewhere. Your members will be able to download exclusive content, tips, job leads, or business advice. If successful, you can even hire assistants and moderators to help you out.

Teaching an Online Class

You can create a course outline composed of modules and worksheets in the form of slides. These can be downloaded for a fee and people can study them on their own. The challenge is in the beginning, as it may take a while to develop a good class outline that can be taught every week. However, once you have set everything up, things get easier. As long as you can make sure that the content on offer is updated and relevant, you can choose to recycle the preceding year's class notes.

How to Sell Your Products

Once you have created your informational product, you need to market it in order to generate enough interest. You will also have to decide how customers will be paying for the products before they download them.

When marketing your informational products, you need to focus on showing the customers the benefits of your content rather than just stating the features of the product. Tell people what they will get from your product and how it is unique. Make sure that your sales copy is easy to read through quickly and use images, bullets, and keywords. Keep your marketing emails short for those people who know you already.

There are certain tools that you can also use to help you sell your informational products:

- SendOwl – This is a monthly subscription platform that charges $9 per month. It is easy to learn and integrates many different payment processors, such as Authorize.net, stripe, and PayPal.

- E-junkie – This is a monthly subscription tool that costs $5 per month. It was one of the pioneer financial platforms for selling digital products. It is cheap if you are just starting an online business, and you can access your money via PayPal.

- Gumroad – This is a service that allows you to channel your customers to a specific page. You also have the option of embedding a link into the product you are selling on your landing page. It is a flexible tool that allows you to tweak the buttons to suit your website, so if you have web development skills, you will enjoy this option. Gumroad enables you to be paid via any of the major credit cards. You can access your money either through PayPal (once in a fortnight) or direct deposit. Since there are no monthly subscription fees, Gumroad is a good option for those sellers who are not yet sure just how many copies of a product will be sold per month. The service only charges you a 5% fee and an additional $0.25 for every transaction made. If you do not feel like committing to paying regular subscription fees, then this is the tool for you.

How to Adapt To Your Market

With time, you will discover that as your customer numbers grow, their needs also change. You should always have your finger on the pulse of your customer's needs so that you know when and how to adapt your informational products. Make adjustments to your products, whether it is by upgrading your course content, updating old information, or adapting to new trends.

If you are writing eBooks about SEO, you need to keep track of how Google adjusts its algorithms. If you are making videos, you could shoot new ones and include upcoming gurus instead of old ones. The key thing is to keep your content fresh. Earning passive income does not mean you have to play a passive role as others pass you by. Keep learning and stay in touch with what your customers want.

Chapter 6: Freelancing

More and more people are looking for new ways to earn more money every day. Having a regular job is not enough to meet today's needs, so freelancing has become one way to make some extra income.

There are a lot of things you can engage in as a freelancer. The beauty of being a freelancer is that you are able to offer your services in whatever area you are passionate about. If you hold a 9 to 5 job, you can use your time after work or weekends to diversify your income streams. With freelancing, you get to choose how to use your time and what to spend it on.

As a freelancer, you will have to determine what your strengths and weaknesses are so that you learn how to hone your craft and make the best use of your skills.

How to Freelance For Passive Income

There are a number of ways in which a freelancer can start earning a passive income. This will obviously depend on the kind of freelancer you are.

Selling Stock

Stock here refers to things like images, themes, scripts, and the like. If you happen to love photography, you can take pictures during your spare time and sell them to stock photography sites. Every time someone goes to the site and buys one of your photos, you get paid. You do not have to be a professional photographer to do this kind of work. With the advancements in Smartphone cameras, almost everyone is an amateur photographer. However, if you want to develop that cutting edge, it would be best if you learned some basic photography skills. Shutterstock is a good example of a website that can earn a good passive income for a photographer.

If you are a programmer, you can start writing scripts and sell them to any of the numerous script websites on the Internet. If you have a passion for web design, you can spend your free time creating templates, graphics, or Wordpress themes. This particular niche is getting more popular every year. It may sound a bit difficult for most people but if you are a designer, you can actually earn a substantial amount if you work on your own products and sell them. You can sell your stock graphics on your own website or to a marketplace. Examples of marketplaces that you can sell your stock themes, templates, and graphics include ThemeForest, GraphicRiver, and Creative Market.

These online marketplaces offer good prices for stocks, and you can make a minimum of $20 for just one template. In some cases, a template can be bought for $300, so the better your template is, the higher the earning potential.

Subscriptions and Memberships

Depending on the type of freelancer you are, you may have a lot of knowledge to share with the world. By signing up to a subscription service or membership area, you can offer your knowledge to customers in exchange for money.

A good example is the Envato network, which comprises a collection of websites and digital marketplaces that allow people with creative assets to offer or sell their ideas to others.

All you have to do is create a tutorial of whatever information or skills you want to share, sign up to the Envato network, and sell your content via their tutorial platform, Tuts+. Customers then subscribe to the network for about $9 per month and are allowed to download whatever content they are interested in. This is a very small price to pay for customers who are looking for high quality content, so if your work is top notch, you earn $9 per month for every subscriber.

Selling Advertising Space

You may have a steady job while also maintaining an active online presence via your personal website. If this is the case, then you should consider selling some of the space on your website to advertisers. This can be a great source of passive income if your website has a huge amount of traffic. Advertisers are always looking to reach greater audiences, and the number of visitors attracted to your blog or website will determine whether they will choose to work with you and how much you can make. As your website becomes more and more popular, you will be able to charge advertisers more money in exchange for posting their ads on your site.

Publish a Book

You do not have to be a writer to put your thoughts and knowledge into words. There are many ghostwriters on platforms like Upwork or Guru who can create a great book for you. Whatever area you are an expert in, writing a book can be a great way to make some passive income. You can self-publish on Amazon or use one of the many eBook services out there, such as e-Junkie.

Design Competitions

If you are into any kind of design, say web design, logo design, or designing flyers, you can enter a design contest. Design contests are not new, and they are a great way for amateurs to create a name for themselves. A design contest website such as 99Designs offers fantastic rates for logos, postcards, or website designs. There is always a design contest going on, so the opportunity to make some money is always available. However, you will have to work hard to make an impression on the contest creator and beat thousands of other competitors.

Chapter 7: Online Surveys

When it comes to making money online, it doesn't get simpler than online surveys. You do not have to make a financial investment or spend too much time setting up a business like the other methods mentioned in the preceding chapters.

Online surveys allow you to get paid every time you complete a survey, and this is something that can be done in tandem with your day job. Unlike a focus group, you do not need to have some kind of specialization to be eligible for paid online surveys. You can also take as many surveys as you like.

How to Use Survey Sites

- You register on any of the numerous online survey sites available. You will need to read the instructions carefully and understand how much you will be paid per survey. Some of the best survey sites in terms of money earned include GlobaltestMarket, SurveyHead, Ipsos, CashCrate, and ValuedOpinions.

- Once you have registered, you will start receiving emails from the survey website. The email will inform you of a survey that you qualify for. You do not automatically qualify for all surveys, and you will only be sent surveys according to the details you filled in during registration.

- Once you complete the survey, you are sent your payment via PayPal, check, coupons and special offers that can be used to buy stuff online.

The Do's and Don'ts of Paid Online Surveys

There are some basic rules that you can adopt to help you make this kind of passive income strategy a success. Some of them may be obvious and you may be knowledgeable about, while others are purely for your safety and security.

The Do's

- Do make sure that you always go to the survey website's privacy policy page and carefully read the fine print. A lot of people skip this step because they want to sign up and start making money really quickly. The danger is that you will never know how your personal information is going to be used, and ho your privacy may be potentially compromised.

- Do find out how much is paid per survey and the minimum payment amount that each site has. This will help you know how much you have to earn before you are allowed to cash out, and how quickly you can do so. There are some sites out there that set very high minimum payment amounts and pay you very little money per survey. When you are close to reaching the minimum amount for cashing out, they suddenly stop sending you surveys. You need to be careful that you don't end up wasting your time and energy on such sites.

- Do create a new email account completely dedicated to receiving emails regarding your paid surveys. You do not want to be swamped in different kinds of emails and fail to see the survey email in time. Some of these surveys are for a specific time frame and you may miss out.

- Do make sure that you check your mail on a regular basis so that your surveys don't pass you by. You can set up desktop alerts for that particular email account.

- Do take the time to update your profile regularly in order to keep receiving the most appropriate or relevant surveys for you. You want to be surveyed on things that you are interested in, and in case your interests change, you will need to update your preferences in your profile.

- Finally, do sign up to more than one survey site. This way, you maximize your chances of making as much money as possible. There will be times when some sites will not be sending regular surveys your way, and having other alternative options will help you go through that dry patch.

The Don'ts

- Do not pay any kind of membership fee to any survey site. Legitimate survey sites offer free sign-ups and do not ask for money upfront. If you come across any survey site that asks you to pay first, move along. They are definitely not legit.

- Do not give out personal information that is sensitive and can potentially be used against you. This includes credit card numbers, phone numbers, social security number, and the like. You do not want to fall victim to some kind of financial scam, or worse.

- Do not let your guard down when it comes to protecting yourself against viruses and spam. Some survey sites can easily expose your computer to viruses or Trojans, so make sure that you have the latest and updated antivirus tools. If you are going to be working online a lot, invest in protecting your computer.

- Finally, do not think that you can get rich and retire by simply filling in surveys. Paid online surveys are a great and easy way to make extra cash on the side, especially if you have the time. However, it is not a way to earn a stable living. Use it, but do not let it b your only source of passive income.

If you want to earn money via paid online surveys, you must have patience and dedication. This is not a get-rich-quick scheme that will make you a ton of money overnight. Be wary of the survey sites you visit and always look for the ones that are trusted and have the best reviews.

Conclusion

Thank you again for purchasing this book!

I hope this book was able to help you to discover just how to start making a passive income by doing what you love. This book has definitely opened up your eyes to the opportunities available.

The next step is to find the best way to monetize whatever passion you have. It may take some time, but you will soon be able to make money in your sleep!

AMAZON FBA FOR BEGINNERS

Proven Step by Step Strategies to Make Money on Amazon

Mark Smith

The information herein is offered for informational purposes solely, and is universal as so. The presentation of the information is without contract or any type of guarantee assurance.

The trademarks that are used are without any consent, and the publication of the trademark is without permission or backing by the trademark owner. All trademarks and brands within this book are for clarifying purposes only and are the owned by the owners themselves, not affiliated with this document.

Table of Contents

Introduction

I want to thank you and congratulate you for choosing this book, Amazon FBA for beginners.

This book contains proven steps and strategies on how to start your Amazon FBA experience. Selling on Amazon through FBA can be a life changing experience. It makes business so easy and simplified that you would have enough time for work and for yourself.

Amazon provides various benefits to anyone who wants to get into the FBA business. You won't find these anywhere else because in essence, Amazon does all the work for you. You also get the opportunity to market yourself to the millions of users that Amazon has.

For a seller in 2016, getting in on the Amazon FBA experience is very important in order expand your business and to learn more about selling online. It's also hassle free. Amazon provides you with step-by-step instructions on how to be a fully-fledged FBA seller. Your only job is to focus on creating innovative products for your customers.

This book will tell you everything you need to know on starting your business with Amazon. I have tried to simplify the procedure so that you are able to understand the basics. There are also numerous tips mentioned throughout this book that will make you an expert in the FBA field.

Without much ado, lets get started!

Thanks again for purchasing this book, I hope you enjoy it!

Chapter 1: Selling On Amazon

In order to understand how FBA works, you have to understand how selling on Amazon works. Amazon has millions of users and is increasing its user base every day. Many people have made a lot of money working through Amazon while others are still struggling. It's also about understand how selling really works on Amazon.

If you want to be a seller on Amazon you have the opportunity of marketing your products in front of millions of active users. You will show up as a third party seller since you're operating your own business. If you open Amazon you will be able to see the list of sellers that sell a particular product. So, it's not just you who is selling the product but tons of people. The customer now has the opportunity to select from all of these sellers.

Amazon allows you to work on a larger scale without going to the trouble of establishing a shop, workers, etc. You can work on whatever scale you want. If you want to sell multiple products then you can do that but if you want to only sell a few products then that's also your choice. If you are simply trying to sell something on the Internet then there might be an issue of scale ability. You might not be able to increase your business on every website. You can function as an independent small seller who is trying to make a little bit of money. It's easy but you don't really get to function as a proper business.

That's what's different about Amazon. It gives you the opportunity to work as an independent small seller dealing only one product or you can be a business tycoon who is handing multiple products through Amazon. This is why selling on Amazon is easy. You don't need huge investments in order to get your business started. If you believe that your product will sell then you can increase the manufacturing. It's extremely risk free. You get the opportunity of making a lot of money without investing a lot. This reduces the risk factor and also helps you to be stress free.

Process

The process of selling on Amazon is easy. Amazon doesn't require much from you. They just need your bank account details and tax information. There will of course be some money that you to pay in order to start your own seller channel but Amazon has some great offers and incentives for new sellers.

Step 1: The first step is to setup your own store on Amazon. You have to register yourself and then you will be required to give a list of the products that you are selling. It's very easy and Amazon provides you with a unique tool that is easy to understand.

Make sure that you do not give any false information and the products that you are listing actually exist. This is the first step in starting your own Amazon business so you should be very careful.

Amazon also has various professional service providers that can help you in creating a unique impression for your product. This is important because you might not know how to really market your product. These professional service providers have been working for years on this kind of stuff and hence, they know the requirements of the market. They will also be able to guide you on how the procedure works. So, it's necessary for anyone who wants to sell their product on Amazon to use the help of such service providers to make sure that you can compete with the world-class sellers.

Amazon also helps you to advertise your products. Amazon's advertisements rules are brilliant. The cost of advertisements through other channels is really high. Amazon only asks for money when someone actually clicks on your advertisement. This is beneficial because you don't have to pay too much. You only have to pay for the real users.

Step 2: The second step is interacting with the customers. It will take some time for your store to go live but when it does you will be able to instantly see the results. Amazon has a collective user base of over one fifty million people just in North America. Globally, there are way too many people who use Amazon daily.

This puts you at an interesting position. You have the option of marketing your product to all of these users without the commitment that is required. You are doing it all online and if it doesn't work out, you would hardly have to deal with loss. This is the best part about Amazon. It's like joining an already built marketplace without investing a lot of money.

If you receive an order from a customer, you will be able to manage it yourself. You will be able to contact the customer if that is what you want or any other information that you might want. It's really easy to understand and the order management dashboard will help you out in whatever you need.

To create a lasting impression on your customers, it's recommended to supply them with high quality products and to also keep focusing on doing it as efficiently as possible.

Step 3: Step 3 is where Amazon makes your life easier. Amazon delivers the product for you. You don't have to do anything at all. Everything is to be dealt by Amazon representatives. You just have to simply supply Amazon with the product and once you are done, the package will be supplied through Amazon and its courier partners. Amazon will come to you in order to pick up the product. The packaging and other logistical stuff is all you have to do.

The shipping by Amazon is really fast and it's also hassle free. This will ensure that you do not lose a potential customer. You will be able to easily get your product to your customer and without any problems. If there is any issue then you can call Amazon at any point and they will resolve the issue for you. If something happens to the product while being transported then it is Amazon that takes the complete responsibility. You can put your complete trust on Amazon.

This is also where the whole FBA business comes in. Instead of just having Amazon pick the product from you, you are given the option of storing your product with Amazon. We'll have a lot of discussion on this later but essentially fulfillment by Amazon aims at reducing your workload. You have to ship the products just once to the Amazon storing facility and they'll keep the product safe for you. Once you get an order, you can direct the Amazon storing facility to ship out your order. You don't have to pack and you don't have to worry about inventory. It makes everything much easier.

This is important because it helps you to focus on your business. You can grow your business and add more product lines while Amazon deals with shipping and other charges. Amazon only takes a little money from you. You don't have to do much. Just sit back and relax.

A lot of businesses have been successful because they have been able to focus on providing customer service without getting distracted by distribution channels. It's essential in the twenty first century because it makes like easier for you. You can dedicate your time on more important things. It helps you to scale your business. If you want to expand your business then you will face the problem of shipping out the products. This can make life very difficult for someone who is handling the business alone. Fulfillment by Amazon ensures that you never have to waste your time with the shipping and packaging business. This allows you to expand your business without putting too much pressure on yourself.

Step 4: Amazon is very prompt with payments. They are an international organization and hence, you won't ever have to deal with payment problems. They deposit the payment in your bank within seven days. The fees that Amazon charges is fair and nominal. They only take fees from you if you make a sale, so they are not exploitative.

Step 5: You can use Amazon to grow your business. Amazon doesn't just ship and sell products for you. It also helps you to be a better businessman or businesswoman. It ensures that you get regular updates about your performance so that you are able to track your progress. Amazon also keeps giving you tips on how to run your business. This will help you to increase your sales and you will be able to make a lot of profits.

It also provides you with regular updates and reports. You will be able to study your performance and see your results. This makes life much easier since you don't have to get any external reporter to make these reports for you. You also don't have to deal with accounting and similar complex activities. You can scale your business as you want and Amazon will be there to help you out.

Amazon is also great for seller services. You can contact them with any query that you have at any point of time without any trouble. It will make everything much easier. You will be able to boost your performance and increase your sales.

Step 6: You can also go global with Amazon. If you wish to expand your business and sell in other countries, you can do so with Amazon. It's really difficult to sell anything overseas. To set up shop in another country and sell your products takes a lot of time and dedication. There are many permits and regional connections that you need. It's almost impossible for an individual seller to sell something abroad without investing in more resources.

Amazon on the other hand helps you to go global without any hassle. You don't need to have regional connections or permits. You can sell online through Amazon and the shipping and other miscellaneous expenses will be handled by Amazon. It's the best way of marketing your products abroad. You get the option of selling on a widely trusted platform and you don't have to invest in anything. You can go global without even getting out of your chair.

Some Tips

If you want to be really good at selling on Amazon then there are certain tips that you have to follow. The main point is to treat selling seriously. You have to innovate and research about everything that you are selling. Think ten times before you decide to sell a product and consider everything related to it from costs to reviews before you decide to sell it. Amazon changes every day and you have to stay on top of the game in order to be successful.

1. If you want to scale your business then you have to use fulfillment. If you were going to spend all of your time on packaging and shipping then you wouldn't have to time to manufacture or find the products that you want to sell. The less you sell the less profits you make. So, if you want to actually make some money through selling, scaling is inevitable. If

Amazon handles the shipping and packaging for you, it'll save enough time for you to just focus on marketing your products.

2. You have to be flexible. Don't just pick a few products to sell and go after them. If a product isn't selling them dump it and move on. You will make a lot of mistakes and incur many losses before you become an expert. If you are not willing to change then you will continue to incur losses. If you see that there are losses in selling a product then stay away from it. You have to make sure that every sale gets you some profit. Be willing to learn. There are numerous experts in the online selling business that are ready to provide you with their services. Take their help without any hesitation. They will tell you all about the new services that are present on Amazon and how you can benefit from them.

3. Manage your inventory. Make sure that everything is noted. Run it like a proper business, even if you are doing it by yourself. You do not want to lose track of your products or money. Take a note of everything and make sure that your inventory is never low. If a customer can't buy your product then you have lost them forever. Keep sending products to Amazon as soon as they are sold. Take care of your cash flow as well. You don't have to hire an accountant but make sure that you don't lose track of the money. Keep tabs on your spending and make sure it all goes as planned. People usually tend to spend way more than they should have. This can create problems while calculating profit margins. Make sure everything goes as planned.

4. If you're not doing well as soon when you started then don't freak out. It's okay to not make huge profits as soon as you start. You have to measure your progress but don't do it too often. Rather work on increasing your sales rather than profits at first. If you have to check your progress weekly then measure

it through sales. Look at the profit and the money on a quarterly or half yearly basis.

Keep your focus on making money. Don't get overwhelmed and focus on the sale that is ahead of you. Try to make as much money as you can on every sale and you will see your progress every time that you check your reports. If you really want to see huge changes then check your progress only after a certain period of time. Don't lose hope and try to innovate as much as possible.

Chapter 2: Fulfillment by Amazon

Fulfillment by Amazon (FBA) is a sales technique. It's the way that Amazon recruits more people to sell their products on its website. The main purpose behind FBA is to give people the opportunity to increase their sales without adding too much pressure on them. You can store your products at the Amazon storing facility and they will send out the product for you. All you have to do is package the product and send it to the storage facility. Then, as soon as a sale takes place, Amazon will send out the product to the required destination and you will be able to receive the money. It has a lot of benefits and most of all it gives you freedom. You can work on growing your business while Amazon deals with the shipping business for you.

FBA does not just stop at shipping. Amazon also provides customer service for you. If there is any problem with the product then you don't have to keep your phone with you at all times. Amazon will deal with the customer for you. This definitely makes selling very easy. For someone who does not have a lot of time and is doing this on the side, FBA is a lifesaver. You can earn some extra money and it doesn't even take a lot of time. It hardly requires any commitment or investment. The benefits of FBA are incalculable.

If you join FBA it also increases the strength of your product. People trust those products that are fulfilled by Amazon. So, the chances of you making a sale also increase. You will be able to sell your products easily and will be able to boost your performance. FBA sellers also get the option of delivering their products in one day. This is very important because a lot of customers buy products from Amazon just for the one-day delivery guarantee. If your product does not come under FBA then the customer won't be able to opt for the one-day delivery option.

Free Delivery is also another feature that comes under FBA. Most customers would never pay delivery charges for a product. FBA sellers get the option of free delivery on all of their products. This makes it easier for your customers to buy the product and get it delivered. The lower the cost of the product, the happier it makes the customers.

It's also been found that most sellers who join the FBA scheme tend to see an increase in their sales. The reason behind this is the aura that FBA has on your products. Most customers are hesitant in buying stuff from online retail stores. If they see that Amazon has fulfilled a product then they are more likely to buy it. It also helps you to establish credibility as a seller. On a site where there are thousands of sellers who are using FBA, if you do not use FBA then there is a pretty good chance you will be lagging behind. To ensure that you are able to deal with the competition, you have to get on FBA right now.

Amazon has world-class resources. There fulfillment centers would be able to take much better care of the products than any other storing facility. They keep the inventory with them so that you don't have to. They also pack the product for you and then ship it. This saves a lot of time for you. Amazon also ensures that their shipping and packaging service are the best in the world. This way, your customers won't have anything to complain about.

Amazon also has a great customer service network. Their representatives are present all over the world and they deal with all kinds of problems. They also provide you with regular feedbacks so that you can change your business strategy accordingly.

Different Types of Sellers

You can sell on Amazon as part of the FBA scheme or as a Merchant Fulfilled Seller (MF). It depends upon you what you want to pick but FBA is what most people recommend. The differences arise in terms of the responsibilities that you will have and the amount of work that you have to do.

If you want to be a MF seller then you have to deal with everything yourself. You won't get help from Amazon in terms of shipping and packaging. You pick a product and it goes live on the website. The customer would not see a fulfilled by Amazon tag with your product and they wouldn't be able to avail one-day delivery either. This is one of the biggest disadvantages that comes with MF. This definitely affects your performance. A lot of customers tend to not have a lot of confidence in products that are not fulfilled by Amazon.

If the customer does decide to buy your product then you will be notified by Amazon to ship the product. You have to take out time from your work to package the product. Once you have done that, you have to purchase the shipping label and post it on the package. Then, you have to personally go to the post office and ship the product to the customer. All of this takes a lot of time and patience. If you have multiple orders then it might even take a whole day to just send out a couple of products. Also, you have to make sure that the packaging is durable and the product is not harmed during transport. If it does happen then you are the one who has to answer to the customer and not Amazon.

A huge issue is shipping through post office. If you do this then you have to charge shipping charges from your customer. This increases the price of the product and there is a pretty good chance that it will lower your sales. Post offices are not exactly famous for being punctual. They might just delay the product and you wouldn't be able to do anything. It's a lot burden and there are many disadvantages associated with it. The only advantage is that you have the freedom of packaging the product as you wish and you might be able to cut down on the shipping cost. Amazon has certain quality checks that make the shipping cost increase by a margin. If you do it yourself then there is a pretty good chance that you saved some money.

But the problem is that FBA makes life so much easier that it makes no sense to be a MF seller. You don't have to package the products again and again. You just have to mail them to the Amazon storage facility and you are done. You don't have to deal with order; the storage facility does that for you. Your customers get the advantage of having one-day delivery. Your sales would definitely increase, as more people tend to buy Amazon fulfilled products than those that are not fulfilled by Amazon.

Amazon also ensures that your product reaches its destination on time. You don't have to worry about your product getting lost and you don't have to directly deal with the customer. You get so much time to grow your business and boost your performance that you will surely recommend FBA to others.

Your product is also featured as a Prime eligible purchase. It means that the customer can pick a better delivery system and get the product faster. It's mostly two days and this ensures that the customer is absolutely happy with the purchase.

You have to pay some part of your sales to Amazon for storing the product and handling the shipping for you. You can also sell as many products as you want because you are not the one who has to worry about packing, processing and shipping. You can scale your business to a huge size without any worries.

Scaling is important because if you list more items for sale, the more money you make. Now, if you are the one who has to deal with packing and shipping then you won't want to scale. It puts too much pressure on you since you can't handle the amount of orders that are coming in. If there is even a little delay then the customer would be unhappy and you might even lose money. You can sell as many products as you want on Amazon because that is your main job. You just have to deal with finding better products to sell on Amazon without wasting your time on the packaging. If there are too many orders then it's the Amazon storage facility, which has to deal with the intake and not you.

You also get a place to store your products. You don't have to worry about maintaining inventory and taking care of it. Amazon hardly charges you for inventory; rather it just takes a part of your sales and only charges for shipping and handling. This saves a lot of time and money.

Chapter 3: Benefits of FBA

FBA has many obvious benefits. If you want to really increase your sales and give a boost to your business then FBA is the way to go. The main benefit is related to how much time you save. You don't have to spend days packaging and shipping products. This makes your business much more efficient.

Amazon has a lot of expertise in the customer satisfaction department and they know what they are doing. If you decide to use their services then you will benefit from their expertise. You just have to pack and they ship it for you. They even handle the returns on the product for you. They take the complaints from customers and forward them to you. They run a virtual business to help you sell more and more while only charging nominal fees.

Grow Your Business

A lot of people want to grow their business and make it better but they can't. They don't have the time and patience for it. It's usually because handling everything yourself can be really difficult. If you are someone who sells products on the Internet then you will have a lot of problem. You would have to handle the logistics of all of your products. Creating product listings and writing out details takes a lot of time. If you have to handle sales along with this then that completely takes all of your time. So, if you have the added pressure of packing and shipping the products to customers then you cannot hope to grow your business.

Amazon allows you to focus on your business so that you don't have to get into the small things. You don't have to waste your time with packing and shipping. You just have to do it once. Just ship everything to the Amazon storing facility and your job is done. If there is an order, the storage facility workers will find your product. Package it and then ship it. They will ensure that the product reaches its destination on time. This gives you the opportunity to expand your business without any boundaries. You don't have to be constrained by anything at all.

Building Trust

Amazon is a huge organization that has existed for many years. Every customer that wants to buy something on Amazon trusts that the product he will receive would be of brilliant quality. Amazon helps in building trust between the customer and the seller.

The FBA sign on your product increases the value of your product. People are more likely to buy a product if they see this sign. There are thousands of sellers on Amazon and it becomes really difficult for the customer to pick just one. The one thing that a customer does know is that they can trust Amazon. So, if they see that Amazon has fulfilled a product they trust the seller.

This is very important to increase your sales. At a place where you can't have any actual contact with the customers, your product page is what determines a sale. So, in order to ensure that a sale happens you have to use the goodwill that is associated with the Amazon brand name.

All Amazon customers trust that Amazon will provide them with high quality services. They trust that the product will be brilliant and they will get it on time. If you have the FBA sign on your product then this trust is automatically transferred to your product.

It's also a fact that Amazon fulfilled products are easier to return since it is Amazon that deals with returns for FBA sellers. This also induces customers to pick FBA sellers instead of non-FBA ones. Amazon also provides the opportunity to be your customer care representative. If a customer has a problem, he can simply call Amazon for help. This way Amazon handles the customers for you.

Costs Less

Amazon ensures that you only pay for the services that you use. You don't have to pay a certain sum to start with FBA. The charges aren't fixed but rather depend on your usage. If you do not use a certain service in a particular month then you don't have to pay for it.

The charges are really flexible. If you use a service only a few times then you pay for the times that you actually used the service. There is also no subscription fee. You can join the FBA scheme without paying anything at all.

Another amazing thing about FBA is that there are no minimum unit requirements. You can ship as many units as you want to the storage facility. You don't have to deal with any pressure with respect to manufacturing.

Amazon even provides you with the option of advertising your product through the site. You only pay for an advertisement if people actually visit your product through it. If nobody looks at the advertisement and you don't get any hit on your product through it, you don't have to pay at all.

Amazon is really great when it comes to pricing. They don't charge for unnecessary services and they don't have any hidden costs. They tell you from the starting what they are going to charge.

When you're sending your product to Amazon storage facility, you don't have to spend a lot of money since Amazon service providers pick the products from your doorstep. You can also pick to send the product to their storage facility by using your own courier service.

Amazon also takes its fee only if you make a sale. There are no fixed charges on Amazon. Amazon only charges some fees if you are making some money. If you are not able to sell anything then Amazon won't charge anything from you.

Customer Service

Amazon handles customers for you. It gives you a space to sell your product so that you can market to millions of customers. It also handles customer service for you.

If you are not selling through FBA, Amazon would take the customer service calls but you would be the one who has to deal with the problems that the customer has. If the customer hasn't received the product then you have to ensure that the product is on time. You also have to deal with tracking. All of this can be really time consuming and painful for someone just getting into the selling business.

Through FBA, Amazon will handle all the customers for you. You won't have to ever take a phone call and deal with customer related queries. Instead, you can focus on growing your business and adding more products.

Returns are really difficult to deal with. You have to deal with the customer then get the product from the customer. It further wastes time and you can't focus on the sales that you might be getting. To ensure that you do not get distracted and can continue your work, Amazon handles the returns for you. You don't have to get the product from the customer; Amazon does it. You don't even have to unpack and catalog the product again. The product goes back to the storage facility it came from and is cataloged again there. This makes your job much easier since you don't have to deal with such logistical issues.

Cash on Delivery

Cash on Delivery has been extremely popular in growing nations. Unlike other countries, these nations still aren't completely dependent on cards. Many still rely on cash and many prefer cash on delivery because of this. Other than that there is growing mistrust for online selling which is why most like to pay only when they have the product in their hand.

Amazon FBA ensures that all of your products are eligible for cash on delivery. This is not something that you can avail if you pick to be a MF seller. That's because sending a product through any postal service is risky and if you use postal service to collect cash for you, you're just playing with your luck. Amazon picks the money for you and deposits it in your account. This way you do not miss out on any customer and you do not miss out on money either.

Prime Eligibility

The best advantage that you'll receive because of FBA is that your product gets Prime eligibility.

Amazon has tried a lot to make sure that people join its Prime accounts. Prime costs a lot but people still spend money to get Prime accounts because of the amount of benefits that they receive because of it. All of your orders are eligible for two-day delivery for free. This is a huge advantage and many customers join Amazon for this particular reason only. There are many other benefits that a Prime customer enjoys but the main one to focus on is the faster delivery options.

If you are part of the FBA scheme then all of your products are eligible for Prime. It means that all of your customers would get their products in two days. This ensures that your customers are satisfied and they keep buying. If you are a customer who wants to buy a product and you don't have the option of getting your products delivered in two days then you would obviously pick another seller.

Amazon itself ensures that people pick Prime sellers. If you look at the sellers available on Amazon then your eyes would definitely go to all those sellers that have Prime written next to them and have two-day delivery. This forces any customer to go for the Prime seller.

So, it's almost a necessity to be part of the FBA scheme if you want to retain your customers. Most customers tend to pick sellers who are FBA rather than MF even if the price is high. This is because being part of FBA adds credibility to your product and your products get delivered in two days.

Being part of FBA is a requirement and not a choice. If you want to be better than other sellers then you have to pick it. You might lose customers due to many other reasons but at least you won't lose them because you didn't deliver the product faster and in a more efficient way. FBA also ensures that you can make huge profits on all of your sales. Amazon cuts down on the excess expenses that you might have made trying to package and ship the product. This ensures that you sell your product in the best way possible.

Buy Box

A buy box is an opportunity for a seller to earn the right to be the one whose product previews if a customer clicks on it. There are various sellers for every product on Amazon, the seller that gets featured in the preview of the product is said to have the Buy Box for that particular product.

Getting a Buy Box is really difficult. Being an FBA seller increases your chances of having a Buy Box. Buy Boxes are really important because they impact your sales. Many people don't even know that there are multiple sellers for a product. They simply buy the product as soon as they open it. This gives the seller with the buy box a huge advantage.

Even though being an FBA seller is not a requirement but to be eligible for a buy box it is recommended to be an FBA seller. It's really hard to get the buy box for any product. So, if you want to get ahead of other sellers or at least be on level ground with them, you have to get FBA.

Chapter 4: Being an FBA Seller

If you think that FBA is the way to go then there are only a few steps that you have to follow in order to become an FBA Seller. You don't really have to do much. If you have a unique product that you make then you can sell it online without any hassle. Even if you don't have any product to sell, you can always use various tricks to come up with unique products. The point is that FBA is a gold mine. It doesn't matter what product you are selling. If you sell it on Amazon then you will definitely make a lot of money. Your profit margins will be huge and you wouldn't require a lot of investment.

Find a Product

If you want to be an FBA seller then you have to find the right product. This is because not all products have a huge online market. Many of them wouldn't sell online at all, like cars or expensive watches. So, you have to make sure that your product is uniquely suitable for online marketing.

You also have to make sure that the product that you pick will be beneficial for you. You have to get the product as cheap as possible so that you can sell it at full price in order to make some profit. The margin should be pretty large because you have to pay Amazon as well for its services.

Now, if you can find a product that you think is correct then great, otherwise you can always use retail products. If you want to earn some extra cash then this is simple. All you have to do is get retail products then sell them on Amazon through FBA to make huge profits. It's a tried and tested scheme. You won't have to do much but you'll still be able to make a lot of money.

The main aim is to find a retail product either offline or online. You have to find the product at its cheapest. So, make sure that you look everywhere before you buy the product.

Look for products that are at selling at discounts. This is so that you can sell the product for full on Amazon and make huge profits. There will definitely be some mall around you that has a discount going on. Look for such places and use them for your own advantage.

Try to look for products with at least 25% discount. This leaves enough room for you to jack up the price and make some nice profit. If a store is having a clearance sale or closing down then it will definitely have the products that you need.

Now, you have to use an app called Scoutify. Scoutify is a brilliant app that lists the current price of a product on Amazon. So, find a store and then go into it with the Scoutify app handy. Scan the barcode of the product with the camera on your phone and Scoutify will pull up the stats about the product. You will be able to see at what price the product is currently selling on Amazon. You will also see how many sellers are selling the product and the bestseller rank of the product. This way you can make some quick calculations to see if you will be able to sell the product on Amazon at a profit.

The main aim is find a product whose price can be increased to make a profit and still the price should be lower than what is currently selling on Amazon. So, you can make out at what cost you should buy the product and what would be your profitability on buying the product.

Now, before you get out there and start selling your products, make sure you test a few products that you have found at home. Fox example, I'll be taking a blue can opener. The aim of this exercise is to show you how to calculate the profit you will make by selling a product.

A can opener is listed at $30 on Amazon. Now, you have to use this app called Amazon FBA calculator. Just Google and you'll be able to use the app since it's free. Just input whatever the calculator wants and you will be able to see the profit that you will make if the can opener sells at this price.

The profit margin is huge on most products. The calculator told me that I could make almost $20 if the product sells. So, if I can somehow find a shop that sells this can opener at $15, I can make $5 profit. If you start looking around in stores you will find a lot of stuff that's still not on Amazon. You can sell these products at even more profits.

Making an Account

If you have finally decided that you do want to sell your product on Amazon then you can go ahead and make an account. So, go to the Amazon site and scroll to the bottom. You will find the option of 'Sell on Amazon' at the bottom left side.

Now, if you are looking to start a serious business then I recommend that you sign up as a pro seller. There are various benefits that you get if you use a pro seller account and if you do actually want to make money in the long run, you will have to pick the pro seller account anyway. It's better to just do it now.

Amazon really values its sellers and hence, it also gives you a free month whenever you first sign up as a pro seller. So, if you think that you don't need the pro seller pack you can downgrade to a simpler account after one month. Amazon does not charge you for the pro account till after the completion of the one-month. It's kind of like a free trial.

As soon as you sign up you also get the free Amazon seller app that you can use to scan products that you find at your home and at stores. The app is kind of like Scoutify except that it is free. If you are a starter then you should definitely use this app since it is simpler to use and you wouldn't be wasting any money.

Tools

There are certain tools that you will require if you want to be a fully-fledged seller. The first basic thing is a computer. If you don't have one, then you can't really become a seller. Your Smartphone can't replace your laptop. You need one to keep tabs of all the orders and to put up your products. Make sure that your laptop is well equipped because if you do decide to sell on a regular basis, it will become your best friend.

Secondly, you will need a Smartphone. There are thousands of apps out there that are really helpful for a seller. If you want to be an expert at what you are doing, then you need that phone so that you are always on the tip of your toes. It also allows you to be better at what you are doing. You can sell your products even if you are out on a vacation and you'll easily be able to upload photos and information about your product even if you're not at home.

You will need a shipping scale. A shipping scale measures the weight of your box. It's important because an increase in weight even by a few grams can cause a lot of problems. This tool will come in handy since your box won't get returned because of it being the wrong size.

A box sizer is important for anyone trying to save money. You can cut down a huge box to the size that you want. This allows your package to be more compact and you don't even have to put something in the filler space. This is a huge problem because packing fillers can take a lot of money. Cut down your box so that it easily fits the product.

Bundle stickers are also important. If you want to send a set to someone then Amazon might separate them. This can be a huge problem because sets have to go together. Bundle stickers tell Amazon that the products are in one set and need to stay together.

Self-sealing poly bags work like magic. If you have to quickly pack something then you can just throw them into self-sealing poly bags and they are ready to go. There are numerous products that can be easily and quickly packed using poly bags.

You can also buy a Dymo printer if you want to save your time. A Dymo printer saves a lot of ink because it is thermal and it also prints item labels on demand so you don't have to wait until the end in order to print the labels.

Dymo Labels are suitable for a Dymo printer. They are water resistant and have a really strong adhesive. This makes them durable.

You also have to buy a scanner. You can buy a Bluetooth one that connects to your computer without any wires. It saves a lot of time and can be carried around easily so that you can scan items while working.

You should also get a bundle of address labels so that the courier service can find the address easily.

Other than that, you need good printers and label makers for your packages. Make sure that you buy this stuff in bulk because you're going to need a lot of it.

Chapter 5: Details of FBA

There are various things to consider when you are selling a product through FBA. There are numerous details that impact your profitability and sales. So, if you're someone who is selling the product without any consideration to the details you will probably have a lot of problems. Consider these small things before you take up FBA scheme as part of your business.

Costs

FBA is not cheap and there are various costs associated with it. If you want to be an FBA seller there are certain charges that Amazon will take from you. This reduces your profit margin and hence, you have to consider the FBA cost before you set the price for the product that you are selling.

The main cost of selling on Amazon is certain percent of your sale. This is something that you have to pay. Amazon is providing you with an online market to sell your product and hence, it is only fair that it takes some money on every sale.

FBA charges are not common for everyone. They are different depending upon the product. The item weight determines shipping cost, handling fees is mostly stable and same for all the products, the picking and packing fees depends on the distance that the Amazon representative has to travel and the amount of material that is used to package the product and storage costs also depend on the amount of space that is covered by the product. This is why it is recommended to sell products that are small. It seriously reduces all of these charges. Larger products take a lot of space and generally require a lot of shipping and packaging charges. You can cut down on the picking up charges by taking the product to the Amazon storage facility yourself. But this is hardly possible for most people since most of the storage facilities are located far away from cities.

You can use the FBA calculator app to see if it would be profitable for you to use FBA. You can't really consider the price of comfort here. Amazon does all the work for you in FBA and therefore, lets you focus on growing your business. This is why it's hard to really calculate if you will profit from FBA or not.

You have to consider cost before you select a product for FBA. You are not being forced to sell all products under FBA. If you find out that you are not going to make any profit by selling a product under FBA, then go ahead and sell that product through MF.

Selling products in bulk usually reduces their cost. If you sell just one water bottle then obviously the cost of selling it through FBA will be too much but if you sell a bunch of bottles, the cost per bottle would be very low. Be smart when you're selling products through FBA. Be aware of the customer demands and don't charge a higher price just for the sake of FBA.

Labeling

When you are sending the product to the Amazon storage service you have to label the product. There are two options that Amazon offers to you for labeling. Both of these options are very different and need to be considered carefully since they impact your sales and profitability. FBA Labeled Inventory involves putting a label on every product that you send to Amazon. This way Amazon can keep track of individual products that you send under the FBA scheme.

FBA Sticker less Inventory involves not putting any label on the package at all. Amazon identifies your product and mingles it with other similar products that are to be sold under FBA. This requires less work since your product does not have to be labeled and also ensures faster shipping because the products can be processed faster in groups.

Try both the methods for different types of goods that you are selling. If you try both the methods you will be able to understand which is better. Both methods costs the same but at the same time one will be suitable for a certain kind of product and one for a certain kind of product. Since sticker less methods clubs products of similar type together you might want to use this method for extremely common products to ensure faster delivery. The labeled method is safer because it's pretty common to see mingling fraud. To ensure that your product is safe, you might want to use the labeled method. You should definitely use the labeled method for products that are expensive to make sure that they are handled with care.

You might also want to consider labeling charges in your profit margin before you pick on any one method for your products.

Product

This is one of the most important parameter when you are trying to set up your FBA business. You have to make sure that your product has certain qualities. You also have to deal with everything related to your product in order to sell it and make a profit.

Make sure that your product is in the range of $10-50. You do not want to go ahead and buy an expensive product because it makes it very risky. There are better chances of being successful through FBA if you sell a cheaper product. Try to go for a perishable product that does not have a lot of uses. This is because customers usually want such products at a faster rate and hence, they look for FBA sellers. Make sure that the product is not too huge or heavy. Since, you have to pay for the storage of the product, it's better to make sure that the product is light and hence, does not cut down on the profit margin.

Go through your competitors. See if any of them have any product that has a rank of less than 5000 in the bestseller category. There are a lot of products on Amazon so if your competitor has some that's in the bestseller category it's better to stay away from that field. Also, try to look for a product that doesn't break easily. You do not want to deal with the loss of even one product. It might impact your profit margins. Make sure that your products are packaged properly when you send them to Amazon.

Check out the reviews of a product that you are going to sell. If a product has a lot of reviews then stay away from it. You shouldn't get into a niche that is already dominated by a certain seller. If there are less than 50 reviews of a product on the first page then the market for that product is mostly open and you can definitely get more customers at a lower price.

If you are making a product then you shouldn't spend too much. The manufacturing costs should only be twenty five percent of the actual sale price of the product. This will ensure that you are able to cover the FBA and other miscellaneous costs and are still able to make a sizeable profit on all of your sales.

Chapter 6: The Procedure

If you want to sell a product through FBA then you have to follow a certain procedure. It's important to make sure that you go through this procedure and understand it completely before you begin selling. Prepare yourself according to this procedure and by the products that you might need in advance. Remember, you can never be too prepared.

Step 1: Give Amazon your Product

In this step, all you have to do is send your product to Amazon so that they can store it for you. You can send in an absolutely new product and even a slightly used product if you want.

Go to seller central. Seller Central can be found in your account and here you can upload your listings. Your listings are your products and this is how your products will turn up on the website.

Amazon will the approve all of your listing or part of it. Amazon has a team of specialists that make sure that only true and high quality products are sold on Amazon. If you're selling good quality products then you won't have any trouble getting approved by Amazon.

Amazon provides you with a PDF that you can print if you want a label or you can also use FBA's label service as an alternative. Then you have to ship the product to Amazon. Amazon provides you with discounted shipping but if you want to use your own carrier and ship the product yourself, then you can use that option as well.

Step 2: Storing your Product

In this step, Amazon receives your product at its fulfillment storing facility and then stores it for you. Amazon will then catalog your product and store in their inventory. Amazon has some great storage facilities where your products are taken care of and are ready to be sent in just a few minutes, whenever it is required.

First, Amazon will receive all of your products and then scan them so that it can keep a track of your products. It also sends you an instant message, informing you that the product has been received.

Amazon then works on storing your product. It checks your product and notes down all of its units. They check the weight, height and other dimensions to find an appropriate place to store your product. It also helps in fixing the cost for handling and storing charges for the product.

Amazon provides you with world-class services. They keep a track of their entire inventory using their sophisticated tracking system. If an order is placed for a product then Amazon is able to find that product quickly so that it can be sent out. They also send you updates about the processing procedure. The tracking system is very effective.

Step 3: Dealing with Orders

In this next step, a customer finds your product and then orders it. Your job is done as soon as you ship the product to Amazon. The order execution is done completely by Amazon and its warehouse service providers. Amazon fulfills the orders that are directly placed on its site and it even fulfills the orders that you request which are not from the website. So, if someone informally asks you for your product, you can ask Amazon to ship him or her the product.

All of your listings are ranked on the basis of price. The price does not include any shipping costs at all. This is because all FBA users have the opportunity to sell their products without any excessive shipping costs.

All FBA products that you sell are eligible for Prime. So, if a Prime customer buys the product, Amazon makes sure that the product is delivered in two days.

If you fulfillment order is not from Amazon then there would be extra shipping costs and the customer won't be eligible for Prime delivery. This is because Amazon provides certain offers only to users that order through the website.

Step 4: Sending out the Product

In the next step, Amazon picks up your product out of its inventory and then packages it properly. Packaging is done again because Amazon makes sure that the product is not harmed and reaches the customer intact.

Amazon first locates your product. The storage facilities of Amazon are all huge. There are numerous products there and yet, Amazon picks up your product in only a few minutes after the order has been received. They have an extremely high-speed web-to-warehouse system. The system keeps a track of all the products and as soon as an order is received, the system locates your product and sorts it out. This system also packs your product carefully.

Customers are also given the option of clubbing their orders for your product with other products fulfilled by Amazon.

Step 5: Shipping

In the last step, Amazon sends out your product so that the customer can receive it. There are numerous products that are shipped from the warehouse everyday and yet, Amazon keeps a tab on all of these orders and sends you updates regularly.

Amazon sends out the product based on the delivery system that was chosen by the customer. If the customer needed the product in one day then Amazon will accommodate that request. The system isn't perfect and sometimes people don't receive their products in one day but this is very rare.

Amazon also provides the customer with tracking information. The customer can login to his/her account and check out where their order is. Amazon also sends similar updates to the seller.

If the order was on the Amazon website, then the customer can contact them if they have any issues. Amazon provides customer care for you. You don't have to talk to the customer directly at all. If there are replacements then Amazon also handles that.

The procedure is really simply and each step tells you about how you can make money by using FBA. So, if you want to use FBA you can simply follow the next steps that have been given below.

Step 1: Go to the Manage Inventory page and there select a product that you would like to include as an FBA listing. You will checkboxes in the left column. Simply select them if you want to sell a product under FBA.

Step 2: Click on the Actions menu and then select Change to Fulfilled by Amazon.

Step 3: Now, on the next page click on the Convert button.

Step 4: Then follow the guidelines given to dispatch your products to Amazon.

Conclusion

Thank you again for purchasing this book!

I hope this book was able to help you to understand the FBA scheme. FBA can be really complex for a first time seller. If you are one then I hope that the book gave you plenty of information to get you started. There are various benefits that come with FBA but there are various problems as well. Make sure that you are smart in your workings and study everything carefully before you start with your very own FBA business. Keep yourself flexible and take advice from wherever you can get it.

The next step is to setup your very own seller account. Go ahead and sell as much as possible on Amazon. Remember to keep a check on your profit margins so that you are able to take complete advantage of the FBA scheme.

Good luck!

AFFILIATE MARKETING

*Proven Step by Step Guide
to Make Passive Income with Affiliate
Marketing*

Mark Smith

Table of Contents

Introduction

I want to thank you and congratulate you for purchasing the book, *"Affiliate Marketing – Proven Step By Step Guide to Make Passive Income with Affiliate Marketing"*.

This book contains proven steps and strategies on how to start off on the extremely exciting and successful journey of Affiliate Marketing Programs. This book gives you a fairly detailed perspective on what is affiliate marketing, how does it work, what is the common lingo you need to learn and master, the importance of creating and maintaining a great blog and/or website, and the top well-established affiliate partners you should definitely sign up with.

I have also dedicated one chapter on the different ways you can leverage your presence and popularity in the social media to back your affiliate programs. Unfortunately, like all things in the world, affiliate programs are also home to a few scamsters and hoodwinkers ready to pounce upon innocent victims and deprive them of money and other valuables. This book has a chapter on how to identify and avoid such dishonest business entities and people.

What is Affiliate Marketing?

The Internet, or the World Wide Web, began its grand growth phase during the 1990s and since then, there has been no looking back for the amazing and ever-expanding technological element. As with the advent of anything new, companies are also looking out for ways to leverage it for marketing. And the Internet was one big unlimited advertising and marketing space for companies small, big, or medium.

Consumers were being serviced in every nook and corner of the world and suddenly for a lot of organizations the size of their target audience grew multifold and continues to grow as more and more people are getting on to the internet especially so in large emerging economies.

The emergence of search engines has added to the power of the Internet and has given rise to a gigantic platform that can support both information and e-commerce. Owners of websites are leveraging on great content to enhance traffic and business owners are riding piggyback on the websites and blogs to enhance their own customer reach and base.

Affiliate marketing is based on relationships and ideally includes three primary stakeholders: the advertiser, the publisher, and the consumer. Let me give you a brief on each of these stakeholders:

Advertiser- In affiliate marketing, an advertiser is anyone who wants to sell his or her products. The advertiser category includes companies looking to sell their products too. The products being sold can range from electronic goods to food items to air tickets to insurance and investment products and more. The critical element here is as an advertiser you must be willing to pay people who help in promoting and selling your product(s) and business.

Publisher- A publisher could be a company or an individual who promotes and sells the advertiser's products and business in lieu of a charge or commission. The advertiser and the publisher enter into a contract wherein the former will provide marketing online materials such as online advertising banners, website links, and text ads which the latter will incorporate into his or her website.

Consumer- The final and the most important party in the triangular affiliate marketing setup is the consumer. The consumer is the one who sees the advertisement and takes action which could include clicking on a link directed to the advertiser's website or filling up a form that the advertiser has requested for. This completion of action by the consumer is called conversion, which is what is tracked for commission payments due to the publisher.

A Brief History of Affiliate Marketing

Affiliate marketing works such that advertisers reward publishers for every new consumer and/or new business transaction that publishers bring in through their own marketing efforts.

The era before the Internet- Although the phrase "Affiliate Marketing" is conventionally an online term, the affiliate concept existed even before the advent of the Internet. For that matter, the concept still exists in an offline mode. A classic example is when your beautician or hairdresser gives you a discount if you refer a friend to her or him.

A huge difference between offline and online mode is that in the offline of old-world brick-and-motor mode, the reach of affiliate marketing is nowhere as wide as that of the Internet mode. Another key difference between the offline and online affiliate marketing programs is that of tracking your referrals. In the online mode, this has been automated and works like a charm and there is not a single converted lead that gets missed out whereas in the offline mode, tracking and getting paid for referrals is quite a logistical nightmare.

The Internet revolution- The Internet is, perhaps, the most profound discovery of the 20th century. It has changed the way we lead our lives. The Internet has influenced every aspect of our lives including advertising. Consumers have started looking for information, opinions, product reviews, and other details on the Internet and hence it has become a powerful tool in the hands of advertisers.

As technology advanced and newer versions of the Internet were released, the effect of advertising could be tracked more easily. With the introduction of cookies in Web 2.0, you could easily check the effect of your advertising campaigns on your purchase funnel. And moreover, the enhanced levels of blogging by consumers, the huge amount of content that is being generated on the web and the opening up of the e-commerce platform was a perfect stage for the onset of affiliate marketing.

The concept of affiliate marketing as is popular today was designed, patented, and implemented for use by William J Tobin. The first affiliate program was set up by W J Tobin for his company, P C Flowers and Gifts. Amazon then launched its affiliate project called Associates Program in 1996 that is considered as an important milestone in the world of affiliate marketing. Amazon's Associate Program garnered far-reaching global interest and many retailers used it as a model to form their own affiliate programs.

Clickbank and Commission Junction opened their affiliate networks in 1998 and with the advent of these networks, affiliate marketing became far more accessible than before especially for smaller retailers. These two networks facilitated exchanges between affiliates and merchants and also offered payment solutions. In 2000, the United States Federal Trade Commission released a set of norms and guidelines for affiliate marketing that gave the online marketing realm a seal of government approval. In 2008, various legislations in the form of new disclosure guidelines and the Affiliate Nexus Tax helped in the streamlining and regulation the field of affiliate marketing.

With the above short history and a basic understanding of "what is affiliate marketing", I would like to reiterate the power of this advertising tool to help you improve your own financial status by connecting you to millions of internet viewers all across the world including bustling, highly populous and cosmopolitan cities like New York, Singapore, London, LA, Beijing, Tokyo and more to the really remote areas of emerging economies like India, Brazil, and the interiors of China.

I hope this book gives you the required charge to help you take off and sustain a highly profitable affiliate marketing program through your social media pages and/or your own blog and website.

Chapter 1: How Does Affiliate Marketing Work?

Affiliate marketing leverages on "cookies," an innocuous and simple technology which was integrated into Web 2.0, to target a specific audience and hence increase the chances of lead conversions greatly. A cookie also helps in identifying, tracking, and avoiding spam and malware and also helps in enhancing the effectiveness of affiliate marketing.

What is a cookie?

A cookie is a technology that collaborates with web browsers to track and store critical marketing data such as user registration and login information, shopping cart contents, and user preferences. I am sure there are numerous times when you have clicked on "Yes" for the computer question, "Do you want your user id and password remembered for this website?" That is an example of a cookie.

Do you notice that when you browsing the web for something, you find a lot of travel based ads and deals coming up on the side? This is because you have been "cookied," that is to say, when you have searched for travel deals earlier, that search has been stored by the cookies and hence target-based ads are hitting other websites that you are browsing. Cookies are great ways to help advertisers track user preferences and send them display banners and consumer deals that match the user's needs. In such cases, wherein what the advertiser's products are perfect matches for the consumer needs, the chances of lead conversions are high.

Cookies track and record the following kinds of information with respect to consumers:

- Website links you have clicked on

- Website ads you have clicked on

- Websites you have visited

- Time and date when you clicked on any link

- Time and date when you visited websites

- What kind of content and websites you like most

When a consumer visits a publisher's website, liked and clicked on the advertiser's website link and/or ad, the consumer's web browser received the tracking cookie and identifies and stores the following information:

- Who is the advertiser?

- Who is the publisher?

- Which is the ad or link that has been clicked?

- Commission amount due to the publisher

All the above information is stored in the link information under the "parameters" field. This field also contains other anonymous data that is employed for attribution.

What are affiliate networks?

Affiliate networks such as Google Affiliate Network, ClickBank, Commission Junction, and more are hubs that connect publishers and advertisers. These networks have the technological wherewithal to track transactions and leads, offer payment solutions and requisite reports. Advertisers, of course, have the option of using these established networks for their programs or employ their own in-house platform.

Let us take a specific link and learn and understand how some of the critical identifiers are used and stored in the link information, which is then used, by affiliate networks and/or advertisers to track and make payments. The following is an example of a link:

```
<a          href="http://www.tkqlhce.com/click-5377085-
10590299?sid=012-123"                    target="_blank">
webservices.cj.com</a><img     border="0"     height="1"
src="http://www.ftjcfx.com/image-5377085-10590299"
width="1" height="1" border="0" />
```

The following features of the link are critical affiliate marketing-based information that you need to know and be aware of:

Publisher website ID (or PID) - In the above example, the PID is 5377085 which is the unique identification of the publisher. A marketing affiliate program usually gives a publisher one unique ID and under that he, she, or the company could have multiple accounts. For example, you as a publisher could have multiple websites all of which could be linked to this unique PID.

As a publisher, you will be able to promote the advertiser's business, services, and products by the display of ads, banners, text links, search boxes and more. Whenever successful leads for the advertiser are generated from your website, you get paid commissions which are usually a percentage of the actual sale or a fixed amount depending on the sale transaction.

Ad ID (or AID) – In the above example, the AID is 10590299 and identifies the specific link. This AID allows the tracking of the performance of the particular link in question and also allows the publisher to get paid commission. Every link has a unique AID allowing for tracking of advertisers appropriately.

An advertiser is also known as a merchant, brand, or retailer and he or she sells a product or service. Advertisers and publishers partner with each other in an effort to increase sales. Advertisers are happier with affiliate programs than other forms of advertisements, as under this scheme they need to shell out commission amounts only on converted leads.

Shopper ID (or SID) - This identification helps the publisher track his or her referred action generators. This data is then used to reward and target shoppers. The visitor's details are recorded whenever he or she makes a purchase and/or completes a lead form. The transaction made is also tracked and stored for reference. Advertisers and publishers depend on shoppers to make a success of their commercial venture.

Working details of an affiliate marketing program

- The various steps and processes that are part of an affiliate program are given below for your easy reference:

- As an affiliate, you first sign up with the advertiser either through an affiliate network or directly. After the contract is signed, you will get a special affiliate URL or link containing the affiliate's username/ID.

- You then use this link for display on your website. Sometimes, the advertiser could send you creative content or banners to appear on your website. These details usually form part of the agreement.

- When a visitor to your website clicks on the advertiser's

link, a cookie from the advertiser is dropped onto the visitor's computer.

- The customer then makes a purchase or does a required transaction on the advertiser's link.

- When the visitor completes the transaction, the advertiser will check the cookie on the computer and find your affiliate ID and give you credit for the transaction.

- The advertiser then updates all relevant reports that reflect visitor traffic as well as sales that your affiliate link has generated.

- Commission payments are made on a regular basis, normally monthly, based on the sales and/or leads generated. These are clearly spelt out in the agreement contract signed by the advertiser and publisher.

Now, that you know and understand what is affiliate marketing and how the processes work, the next chapter deals with commonly used lingo in the affiliate marketing world. This will help you know exactly what your contract terms are and how and when the payments are made.

Benefits of Affiliate Marketing

Affiliate Marketing has become so important in the last few years that in many industries it has predominantly replaced offline marketing. In affiliate marketing, you do not need to invest any time and effort in creating a product or service to sell. Once you have a platform to sell a product or service, you can start selling those products or services.

Companies and individuals can utilize the power of affiliate marketing to earn profit from each sale they are making. Other than these, here are the other benefits of affiliate marketing:

Outsourcing

Most affiliates are experts when it comes to search engine marketing, which will provide you with the chance of getting to the top of search engines like Google or Yahoo without the need to spend too much money on Search Engine Optimization.

Affiliate marketing is one of the fastest ways for small companies to be exposed to the market since advertisements can be placed on various websites. Businesses can also save time in affiliate marketing since there is no need to search and find potential customers anymore.

No Fixed Hours

When you start affiliate marketing, you are also the one setting up your own working hours. When you work for a boss, you work when they tell you. There might also be times when they will ask you to work after your working hours just to have a job done.

Working at your own time means you can choose the ideal time when you think your body will be at the peak of its concentration. If your peak time is from 6 in the morning until 10 in the morning, then you can work during those hours. You may just choose to resume your work again in the afternoon, during peak hours again. If you are working for a boss with a dictated timeframe, you cannot choose to work with your body, which may affect your work nonetheless.

Only Incur Fixed Costs

There is no budget wasted when it comes to affiliate marketing. The amount paid to the affiliates is the cost of sale. The business owner will set the bounty and they will only pay when sales are made.

Find-ability

Once a consumer visits search engines like Google and Yahoo, multiple listings will be directed and linked to the business, which will provide a better chance of being found compared to the other competitors who only have one to two links on the first page.

Visibility

High search engine listings can be secured by the affiliates and they can display advertisements on their websites. In referring customers, an affiliate only needs a website. This is free brand, product or service exposure that does not have any down time.

Better prospects and acquisitions

The affiliates can choose the ads they wish to use and advertise on their websites. These affiliates know who their audiences and future clients are. Because of this, they can pick the campaigns most suited to attract these prospects to their demographic. It is based on the affiliate's interests to pick the ads that the audience will mostly likely respond to.

Cost Effective

Affiliate Marketing is the most cost-effective when it comes to direct marketing options. Other direct marketing options like multimedia, billboards and pay-per-click advertising may be effective but are also expensive. There is no budget wasted when it comes to affiliate marketing since no payment is needed to be given to an affiliate unless a visitor becomes a customer.

Chapter 2: Commonly Used Lingo in Affiliate Marketing

Before venturing out on anything new, learning the basic communication skills is critical to making a success of the venture. How the various aspects of a new business are named, what the names mean, what words do the various stakeholders use to communicate with each other, code language used; all these elements are extremely important to learn and master before you plunge into a new business AD-VENTURE.

Being familiar with terms that are used in the business helps you gain confidence when you are speaking to people associated with the business. This improved confidence aids in improving the success of your venture. Using the same lingo puts you on par with the experienced in the field and enhances your confidence level significantly.

This chapter is dedicated to helping you learn the commonly used terms and lingo in affiliate marketing. I have arranged the words and phrases alphabetically to facilitate an easy search. So here goes:

Above the fold – This is that part of the website or blog which a visitor views without scrolling down. This part is the first thing to be made visible when the page loads.

Adware – Many times referred to as spyware, this is usually part of free software in which unnecessary and annoying advertisements are included. Moreover, many times, these software programs are difficult to uninstall and can create a lot of nuisance for consumers. Established advertisers normally do not want to associate themselves with affiliates who use this rather deceitful method of advertising.

Affiliate Agreement – This is a contract sent to you whenever you initiate a new relationship with a merchant and/or affiliate network. It is a legally binding document that contains rules, regulations, responsibilities, expectations, and other critical legalities concerning both sides of the affiliate partnership namely the publisher and the advertiser. It is the terms of service between the two parties, which oversees and defines the affiliate relationship.

Affiliate Link – This is the unique link provided to you at the start of the relationship by the advertiser. This unique link identifies you as the affiliate whenever traffic from your blog and/or website is being directed to the advertiser's website. This link helps to track the sales and traffic generated by your marketing efforts. The affiliate special link or URL is embedded with the affiliate's username and/or ID.

Affiliate Managers – Affiliate managers are people who help advertisers manage their affiliate programs. These people carry the onus to recruit affiliates, ensure affiliates are promoting their products and services in a legitimate manner, and to increase sales from affiliates. Affiliate managers are usually a bridge between the affiliate and the advertiser. They could either be in-house employees of the advertiser or offer services as third party vendor such as affiliate networks.

Affiliate Network – Affiliate networks are third-party service providers that help advertisers manage their affiliate marketing programs. These networks help connect the advertiser and the affiliates thereby enhancing the advertiser's reach. They also offer the required back-end technological support to keep track of and record and deliver reports regarding traffic and sales generation leads created by the publisher. They also ensure that the publisher is paid correctly and as per the signed contract.

Affiliate networks facilitate the enhancement of available programs both for the advertiser and the publisher on a common platform. Some very popular affiliate networks that operate in the market today are Commission Junction, Amazon Associates, and ClickBank.

Affiliate Program – An affiliate program is one that is offered by advertisers to publishers wherein the latter refers people to the products and services of the former. The advertiser pays a predetermined commission to the publisher in return for the said referrals. Affiliate programs are also referred to as partner, associate, revenue, or referral-sharing program. Many advertisers use their **in-house** affiliate programs that are referred to as **indie programs** the full form of which is "independent affiliate programs."

Approval – Merchants or advertisers give either manual or auto approval to partner with affiliates. **Manual approval** entails the advertiser to look at each application individual and give his or her approval for the affiliate's participation in the program. **Auto approval** means that the advertiser approves all affiliate applications instantly and automatically.

Banner Ad – Banner ads are visual graphical ads of the merchants that are displayed on the publisher's website.

Charge Back – There could be times when a customer referred by you buys the advertiser's products and/or services but cancels the order later on. During the interim, the advertiser may have paid your commission. On cancellation of his order, the advertiser will deduct the amount of the commission paid to you and this deduction is called charge back.

In those affiliate programs which pay for lead generation, this charge back can be triggered if the advertiser feels that the referrals are fraudulent.

Cloaking – Cloaking is obscuring content from a webpage or it could also entail hiding affiliate tracking codes within links. Content hiding is against prescribed norms whereas hiding tracking codes is allowed and is commonly practiced in the field of affiliate marketing for increased click counts and other marketing advantages.

Click Fraud – There are many affiliate programs that pay based on pay-per-click. In an attempt to get paid more, there are many people who merely click on the said link without having any real interest in the advertiser's products and services. These fraudulent clicks never get converted into sales and hence are referred to as click frauds.

Commission – This is the amount of money received by the affiliate from the advertiser for providing referrals and/or sales leads. This amount is usually a predefined element that is paid if the desired outcome is realized by the advertiser owing to the marketing efforts of the affiliate. Commissions are sometimes referred to as **customer bounty** too.

Contextual link – This is a link that is embedded within the content of your blog or website as against being put in the sidebar which is a more conventional form.

Conversion – A conversion is said to be achieved if a visitor to your website has clicked on the advertiser's link and has completed the required action plan such as signing up for the advertiser's website or purchasing a product. Conversions are dependent on the desired result and will vary from advertiser to advertiser. This element is usually included in the affiliate agreement.

Cookies – Though this term is not exclusive to affiliate marketing, the advantage of cookie technology is leveraged by affiliate marketing programs to track and record sales and transactions triggered from the publisher's domain. Cookies are used to assign unique IDs to various users to keep track of conversions and payments.

An example of how a cookie works is given here. Suppose you had written a book review on your website along with a link to buy the product from Amazon. A visitor views the book reviews and clicks on the link to buy the book. However, for some reason, he or she was not able to complete the transaction. After a couple of days, the visitor goes directly to Amazon and buys the book. Since the cookie had already been inserted by Amazon into the visitor's computer when he or she clicked the affiliate link from your website, you will get the commission for this purchase as the sale is attributed to you despite the fact that the visitor bought the book later on and without coming to your website again.

Cookie Retention/Expiration – Every cookie comes with an expiry date after which the cookie gets dropped from the customer's computer. If the customer chooses to complete the purchase after the cookie is expired, the sale is not attributed to you. Usually, the cookie is retained for 30-90 days; however, there are some wherein the duration of retention is much shorter.

Cookie Stuffing – This is a sneaky way to get more sales attributions by unscrupulous affiliates. Cookies are deliberately and sneakily inserted from the advertiser's website to the consumer's computer without the user actually visiting the affiliate's website. This method is done based on the fact that someday the consumer would visit the advertiser's site and make the purchase that would then be attributed to the affiliate who had sneaked in the cookie.

This kind of underhand dealing is frowned upon by all legitimate users and these kinds of affiliates are also banned from many programs. So, it is important to know such underhand dealings do exist and there are ways and means to catch and ban the culprit. Never ever indulge in this method of unscrupulous affiliate marketing!

CPA – The full form of CPA is Cost Per Acquisition/Action. This is what the advertiser pays the publisher based on the qualifying action taken by consumers that are directed from the publisher's website. Commonly used actions include sign-ups and completed sales.

CPA is sometimes referred to as CPO (Cost Per Order) or CPS (Cost Per Sale) and refers to the amount paid by the advertiser to the publisher for every qualifying order or sale.

CPC – The full form of CPC is cost per click and as the name suggests, refers to the payment made by the advertiser for every click on his or her online ad that is displayed on the publisher's website.

CPL – The full form of CPL is cost per lead and again as the name suggests, it is the amount paid by the advertiser to the publisher for every qualified lead which could be in the form of email ID, completed registration forms, a survey form, or any other as described in the affiliate agreement.

CTR – The full form of CTR is Click-Through Ratio/Rate that is a metric normally employed in direct selling advertising. This ratio represents the percentage of visitors to the affiliate's site who have clicked on the advertiser's link.

Datafeed – Datafeed is a file containing all product details of a particular advertiser. The details include descriptions, images, and prices of the products along with your affiliate link. Datafeed is highly useful when you are establishing an online store that features affiliate products.

Disclosure – A notice or page on your website telling your visitors that you are being paid or compensated for buying products, service endorsements, and recommendations made by you is called disclosure. This is in accordance with Federal Trade Commission laws.

EPC – The full form of EPC is Earnings Per Click that is the average income you earn as an affiliate for every click. To calculate EPC, you would need to divide the amount of commission earned by the total number of clicks on the affiliate link. Here is an example to illustrate EPC: suppose you have earned $4000 as earnings in the entire lifetime of your affiliate membership for a particular link and the total number of clicks is 12,000, then the EPC would be 4000/12000 = 33 cents.

First Click – This is one way in, which an affiliate program works. Let me explain this term with an example. Let us assume that a visitor came to your site and clicked on the advertiser's link but did not make the purchase that time. After some days, suppose this visitor went to another affiliate's site, clicked on the same advertiser's link and makes the purchase.

This advertiser attributes this sale to you because the first click to the advertiser's website was from your link. However, this transaction must happen within the cookie expiry date. To reiterate, since the first click to the merchant site was from your site, you are given attribution for the sale providing it is completed before cookie expiry date.

Last Click Attribution – This is another way an affiliate program works. This is the opposite of first click is last click attribution. Whichever site the consumer last visited and clicked on the advertiser's website is given the attribution for the sale, if any. In this case, the earlier clicks are ignored and only the affiliate site from the last click happens is taken into consideration.

Impression – Impressions measure the number of times an ad is displayed on a page. Each time an ad is displayed is equal to one impression.

Master Affiliate Network – Using a JavaScript code that is appropriately placed on your site allows you to link to some or all merchant affiliate programs through a master affiliate network. SkimLinks and VigLink are examples of popular and established master affiliate networks.

Niche – A website that deals with a specific vertical or topic is called a niche site. For example, if your blog is dedicated to cookery, then it would be designated a niche website.

Payment Threshold – Many advertisers require affiliates to accrue a minimum amount threshold to make the commission payment. This limit is called the payment threshold.

PPC – The full form of PPC is pay per click and this payment model entails that the advertiser should make commission payments for every click on the affiliate's advert. Also referred to as cost per click or CPC, this payment model is used by many established advertisers and affiliate networks.

ROAS – The full form of ROAS is Return on Advertising Spend and it is a term used to calculate the revenue received for every dollar expended on advertisements. It is a ratio got by dividing the generated revenue by the cost of advertising and campaigns.

ROI – The full form of ROI is Return on Investment. In simple terms, this is calculated by evaluating the profit (or loss) made against the amount of money invested in the business. The invested amount would be a sum of amounts used for setting up the business, advertising costs, running costs, and more.

PPS and PPL – Pay per sale and pay per lead are commonly used payment methods in the affiliate marketing field.

Privacy Policy – A page on your website should be dedicated to letting visitors know how you will deal with the private information that they will be giving you via contact forms or through hidden tracking methods. This disclosure norm is a prerequisite to participate in many advertisers' affiliate programs. It is also needed to partner with Google Analytics and Google Adsense

Super Affiliates – The highest earners in any affiliate program are known as the Super Affiliates and normally these people contribute up to 80% of total sales generated by the program. Most advertisers love to partner with super affiliates as this frees up their time to focus on their core competencies as the affiliate marketing tactics are anyway working wonders.

Super Affiliates normally enjoy the power of **co-branding** offered by the merchants wherein the link from the affiliate takes the visitor to the landing page of the advertiser, which contains the brands of both the affiliate and the merchant.

Tracking Code – The tracking is the unique ID given to you by the advertiser when you first sign up the affiliate agreement. This tracking code helps keep track of traffic, sales, and leads generated by you as an affiliate based on which commission payments are made.

White Label – There are some advertisers who allow their products and/or services to be sold by the publisher under his or her own brand. The consumer gets the impression that the product actually belongs to the publisher. This is referred to as white labeling.

Now, that the common and a few uncommon terms are clearly explained to you, the next chapter specifically deals with how important it is to have a great website or blog so that you can attract more visitors and hence enhance the business and marketing opportunities through your blog.

Chapter 3: Blog/Website – A Key Element for Affiliate Marketing Success

Starting and maintaining an epic blog or website is perhaps the most important element to take care of if you are looking to make your affiliate marketing venture a success. If you desire to monetize your blog, then simply putting together and updating a few posts and then hoping for the best in not enough at all. You need to put on your thinking cap, work hard, and create an excellent blog that will attract and retain loyal readers and then rake in money and success for you.

Before you set up your blog, you must know what your niche is, what you are going to write on, and where your traffic is going to come from. You will have to sit down and do some serious research and find a profitable niche that you can write about such that you increase traffic to your blog and then monetize it. The following steps will help you start off a great blog:

- Pick a niche

- Register a suitable domain name

- Get a good web hosting plan or

- Install a popular and well-established blogging platform such as WordPress, Jekyll, Tumblr, etc.

- Create Great Blog Content

How to choose a niche that is profitable for you?

This is, I believe, the most important element in creating a blog that will slowly but surely bring in more traffic and hence deliver unlimited business opportunities. Choosing a wrong niche can be the beginning of the end for you in blogging. Despite beautifully written content, a wonderful blog design, and great pictures - if the right niche is not chosen, you will not succeed in monetizing your blog.

There are various ways to find the most profitable niche and here are some of them:

Follow the money trail – Look out for those niches wherein companies are spending the most amount of money towards advertising. This method is the most sensible way to find your profitable niche because companies will not be spending that kind of money unless they are sure Returns on Investment are coming by boatloads.

How do you find a profitable niche using this method? Simple! Use Google Keyword Planner and search for the keywords using a search such as Google or Bing. If there are more than 3 or 4 advertisements coming up on the side for the same keywords, then you can be sure this is a profitable niche to take up.

Google Keyword Planner will again help you find what the average price of a click is for that niche and you will be able to estimate the earnings you can make from Google Adsense.

Another way to find a profitable niche is to leverage information from Spyfu; a fairly accurate search analytics tool. Spyfu gives you the keywords and key phrases that advertisers are paying for and how much. Commission Junction (CJ.com) will also help you find a niche that is profitable.

Facebook – Facebook, other than being the world's biggest social media network, is also a very useful tool to find out if the niche you want to choose has the potential to make you money or not. Create and follow your Facebook Page to know and understand your fans better. Learn about their profiles, their likes and dislikes; use suggestions from Facebook to check out competition etc.

Old-world Keyword Research – Despite the seeming antiquity of this method, believe me, it works really well to decide on a profitable niche. With the right key phrase you can garner a lot of information based on which you can choose to or leave out the niche you are researching:

The level of competition – more the number of searches; higher the demand for the niche

Name of relevant brands and companies

Intentions of the searchers – Invariably people using the widget review are people keen on making the purchase. Phrases such as "widget name and number," "top widget brands," "buy widget online," etc. indicate a better chance of completed sales whereas phrases such as "complain widget," "widget history," etc. have lesser chances of completed sales.

Register a suitable domain name

Here are a few tips to help you choose a good domain name:

- Stick to .com as most searches are done with .com rather than other options such as .net, .tv, .info, etc. The .net option is a good one too, but try and get the .com option

- Keep your domain name short, simple, and sweet

- The domain name should be easy to spell and

remember. Avoid complex and obscure words and phrases.

- Avoid hyphens in your domain name

- Remember to include the keyword in your domain and keeping it at the beginning of the name is better than keeping it at the end. For example, if "flying bats" is the keyword, then a domain name like flyingbatsaregreat.com is better than comeseemyflyingbats.com

- Do not be depressed by the fact that the "perfect" domain name you chose is already taken; come back to the drawing board and start again. Remember perseverance pays.

Get a good web hosting plan – There are many web hosting services companies available in the market. The top established hosting sites with a proven track record include Go Daddy and Blue host. Visit their websites and choose a plan that suits your needs and wallet the best.

Install a popular and well-established blogging platform

There are many people who recommend the use of your own website via a web hosting service instead of using a free blogging platform. As there are advantages and disadvantages for both, you can do research and make suitable choices. Here is a list of some popular free blogging platforms that are used by people all across the world:

WordPress.Com – This free blogging platform (any upgrades come at a cost) is, perhaps, the most popular blogging platform in the world today. WordPress works really well for those not wanting customizations and added plugins. It is a great way to test and strengthen your blogging skills here without having to spend time and money on your own blog.

Tumblr – Again, a free blogging platform, Tumblr is easy to set up. You can start blogging immediately and the "reblog" function of this platform is a great tool.

WordPress.org – The main difference between WordPress.com and WordPress.org is the former is hosted on the server of WordPress whereas the latter is hosted on an external server. There is a small hosting cost for WordPress.org and gives you access to a wide repertoire of themes and plugins that will enhance the profile of your blog immensely!

Create great blog content

Content is king is the oldest and yet the most timeless adage that rings true irrespective of the platform that we use. And nothing is farther from the truth even in making a great commercial success of your blog. Here are a few reasons as to why content was, is, and will continue to be king and why you need to focus on this extremely critical element of your blog:

Great content works wonder for SEO – Original and high-quality content on a website has a large impact on SEO rankings. Regularly published unique content with links to other relevant content along with keywords placed naturally in the text automatically enhances the SEO ranking. A better ranking means more traffic to your blog and hence increased business opportunities too.

Great content enhances visitor engagement – If you write good content, visitors will flock to your website as they will feel more engaged with your writing than with a badly written content. Visitors will be encouraged to leave comments, like, or even share your content thereby enhancing your brand. Another great way to ensure your content to start off well and foster a great consumer relationship is to make sure your content is available on social media too and can be easily shared.

Great content generates sales – When you are content is unique, honest, and transparent, people are more likely to believe what you say and what you display on your pages. This exhorts them to make purchases and click on affiliates' ads on your website thereby leading to increased leads and sales which in turn translate to more money for you. Moreover, the spread of your brand by word of mouth will increase traffic too.

Great content adds value to your readers' lives – Value adding content more often than not is liked by consumers as invariably their daily lives are impacted positively. Educative content such as good, honest product and service reviews, how-to blogs, learning-based videos go a long way in attracting and retaining loyal visitors to your website.

The quality of your blog content has a direct impact on the way you make your earnings through affiliate marketing programs. Do not ever underestimate the power of creating good-quality and unique content. Make sure you update content regularly and thereby increase the chances of making more money via the affiliate marketing route.

Chapter 4: Affiliate Marketing Strategies

Affiliate marketing has undergone tremendous changes since its first appearance in the world of Internet. A lot of regulations and laws have been set up; SEO rankings are fairly ruthless in discarding and punishing thin and low-quality content; there are huge challenges as competition is gaining ground; it is getting really tough to stay ahead in the game of affiliate marketing.

Despite the difficulties, this realm has a lot of opportunities in store and if you work hard and diligently and persist in your endeavors, you are bound to find success. There are many people out there who are making millions through the affiliate marketing channel. There are simple, straightforward, and honest strategies that will help you gain ground here and this chapter lists a few critical and important ones for you:

Stick to a small niche and delve deep

Many first-timers make the common mistake of working with multiple niches and not having the focus to work hard only a couple of them. Instead of creating multiple websites covering many topics, choose 2 or 3 profitable niches and work hard at each of them to increase traffic and garner more sales and leads.

Once you have achieved some amount of success, then you will find the resources to handle more number of niches across various topics. But in the beginning work at a couple and delve really deep instead of only scratching the surface of many niches.

Newcomers to the system often make the mistake of peppering their site or sites with lots of different things, imagining that people are likely to buy more because they have more choice. It is typical human thinking to want a lot of choice in anything and everything, let alone links on a website. But then, this is wrong on so many levels. You are not a store – you don't have to offer your customers choice because they did not land on your site with purchase in mind. They're there for information, and if you're good at what you do, you'll be able to persuade them to buy something while they are there so you can make some cash.

Think of it as a classy gig to have only one website promotion and that website is the best one that your readers can have. That is, you will have the chance to promote one product or service better rather than having to do it for 5 or 6 different ones. Not only will that confuse your customers but it will confuse you as well. You will have to look into two or three different companies and think of where their links will look the best. So in effect, you will be complicating the process for yourself. It is better to have faith in one product or service and promote it to the best of your abilities. Think of yourself as a pop-up store to promote one product as opposed to a supermarket that offers a lot of choices.

Say there is a camping website. In this instance, it would be a good idea to affiliate with a business that retails camping and leisure goods, rather than a single product. Say you write a review article on the latest winter sleeping bags. You can point out the virtues and problems of a product sold by your affiliate, and if you pitch it right, they'll want to buy one. Because they can do it easily from your site, they'll click, and maybe buy something else as well while they're at it.

It is always the power of suggestion that works on a majority of the customers. They will take a liking to something if you tell them that you are offering them the same product that you have personally tested and liked yourself.

On the other hand, if there's too much choice – say you've got links to half a dozen different sleeping bags, as well as the one you've reviewed – they'll go to a price comparison site to check things out. Once they leave your site, it's unlikely they'll return, so you've lost the sale – and the commission. So don't make the mistake of putting up too many choices at once. If you have put up just one and the website is offering it at the best price in the market then even if the person has left your site to do a quick price comparison, he or she is sure to return back to your site to click on the ad.

So, stick with one business or product. If you want to do more, set up a different website for each affiliate, and concentrate on that, rather than spreading yourself too thinly.

Create superior content

A huge challenge that you face as an affiliate is to instill confidence in your visitors and provide value to them. While large companies spend a lot of money creating brands, you have the power to sit down and create such superior content that it would be nearly impossible for search engines not to direct traffic to your site. Spend time and energy to create and update great and engaging content that your visitors will love to read, like, and share. Nothing sells better than word-of-mouth praise from loyal visitors.

Make your site a brand by itself

Many large affiliates in the market started off small and yet with hard work and perseverance, they have been able to create a brand for themselves. This kind of brand building happens with consistent quality content, strong and powerful editorials, and value additions that they offer customers.

Ensure your affiliate programs include recurring revenues

Marketing strategies are extremely fluid in the affiliate realm and what works today need not work tomorrow driven by multiple factors including changes in the ranking algorithm, affiliate programs shutting down, cost cutting in advertising, and more. It is prudent to ensure that some of your revenue is based on recurring revenue even if it means getting paid in smaller amounts but more frequently. While one-time payments are great to increase revenue, they do not offer protection against major changes that could negatively impact your earnings from affiliate programs. It makes sense to slowly build up a recurring revenue foundation within your affiliate program portfolio.

Ensure your visitor traffic is from multiple sources

If you rely only on one source for your traffic, then when that dries up or some drastic changes take place, then your entire affiliate program will come crashing down. So ensure that your content is viewed across multiple platforms thereby enhancing traffic diversification and reducing risk due to the unexpected downfall of a single source.

Make sure your content is good for mobile devices

The usage of mobile devices has grown in leaps and bounds and relying on any technology that does not support these devices is a sure short way to lose out on plenty of business opportunities.

Preempt breakout trends and prepare well for seasonal trends

There are hundreds and thousands of new and emerging breakout trends on the crest of which smart affiliates ride on and make their money before they ebb out. It is critical that you preempt these breakout trends much before and take advantage of them before customers' interests begin to wane. Google Trends is a great way to check for upcoming breakout trends and get ready to cash in on the flood.

Seasonal trends, on the other hand, are easier to predict because they recur regularly and you will know the rise, the peak, and the downward slide well. This will help you prepare for seasonal trends too. These preemptions and preparations will guarantee that you do not lose out on any great opportunity to make a success of your affiliate program.

Participate in affiliate programs that enhance your affiliate income by magnitude

While small value commissions from large traffic inflow are good initially, as you grow and evolve in the affiliate market field, it is important to promote high-value products that will give you increased income per approved lead or sale. Increasing the value of the products you promote is easier than having the increase the traffic inflow multiple times.

Create content that meets changing SEO requirements

As Google is getting more and more sophisticated with its SEO technology and including similar terms to match with keywords, it is important to create content that is in sync with these changing needs. It makes more sense now to have in-text content that is more relevant to readers instead of simply focusing on keywords. Hence, target topics appropriately instead of keywords and phrases.

You must be well versed in the concept of "SEO." SEO refers to search engine optimization. You must have heard that many companies have a good SEO team that helps them to increase their popularity. Well, this is true because these teams work hard in promoting the websites and blogs of the company and help it appear on top of the Google search list.

For this to happen, you need to pick out all the top words from your blog or website, that are most likely going to be typed into search engines by people. If they get the combination of words right then your site is going to appear as the topmost link. For this, you can also make use of a small description that will help you put in all the main words on your site. But remember just a good SEO description will not do the trick and you need to have good content as well.

Promote products that you are very familiar with

Marketing products that you are familiar with has many positives. The first is that you are comfortable talking about its benefits and uses and this confidence comes out in your content. The confidence that is reflected in your writing is invariably felt by the readers and people who want to buy the product will be compelled to do so.

Secondly, there is a sense of satisfaction you will feel that you have been able to convince someone else based on your own experience and hence your feedback is genuine and not misplaced. Such honest marketing strategies will definitely bear fruit sooner than later as the integrity of your recommendations is bound to spread by word of mouth slowly but surely.

Product Review Sites

A classic form of affiliate marketing is to build a product review site that you keep updated regularly with reviews and recommendations of products that you have used. Featuring links to the product's website either on the sidebar or including in the content is a great way to compel customers to buy the product immediately after reading your well-written review. If the review is honest and straightforward your affiliate marketing income will grow by leaps and bounds as you keep adding and updating your site regularly.

Use blogroll or Partner Center

Affiliate links can be placed on a website as a logroll or partner center. The blogroll contains affiliate links to multiple third-party sites that are also blogs. However, these links take visitors to a landing page wherein they can sign up for a product and/or service.

Sites that Aggregate Product Feed

These kinds of sites are also great for affiliate programs. You, as the publisher, would aggregate various kinds of information regarding products and upload it onto your site. The details would usually include images, prices, and specifications of the product. This kind of compelling information and hard facts about the product could drive the customer to click on the link on your site to purchase the product.

Work on your Website First

Affiliate marketing thrives on people's interest in clicking on links to products that catch their eye. But who are these "people"? Well, these are people who will visit your blog or website to read what you have written. So in order to lure these people, you have to make your blog or site as interesting as possible. It is fine to go all out and decorate it as much as you like. But make sure you stick with the intended theme otherwise, people will only visit to mock your blog.

Remember that you need to establish a good reader base in order to land an affiliate marketing gig.

So, it's no good setting up a website today and joining an affiliate marketing program tomorrow. Until you're getting a good number of unique visitors – or impressions - to your website, you're not going to get the click-through to your affiliate. Here, "unique" refers to new customers and not the same old ones who have probably bookmarked you and keep visiting all the time. You must have had several of your friends telling you to check out their blog or site and also who have asked you to visit often and spread the word. Well, they are doing this so that their site or blog has enough "traffic."

Clearly, not everyone is going to click on the links and to get a reasonable amount of clicks, you need plenty of regular visitors. You also need to build up a reputation as an expert in your niche before people will trust you enough to go for your recommendations. It is like running a site that throws up one interesting piece of writing after another in order to lure people into reading it and staying put. That is exactly how your website should operate. There should be interesting content for people to read and remain glued. It is not helpful if they visit just once and immediately forget about your blog.

You need to track the number of people that visit your page and record the numbers per day, per month and per year. This will help you in knowing how popular your blog really is.

So what happens when you have enough visitors? Before you

ask, nobody seems to be sure what constitutes 'enough' in this case. Some people say 1,000 impressions a month; others say 1,000 impressions a week. So it is safe to assume that having at least 4000 to 6000 impressions a month will help you in becoming popular enough. Well, then you have to be patient because it will take time to build up revenue. Remember that it is always cumulative and for the number to go high, you need to wait it out. You're not going to be making $ 1,000 dollars while you sleep at the end of the first week. In fact, it could be months or even years before you get to that stage if you ever do. And you certainly won't pull in the big bucks with just one website. Play the patience game, and take the time to learn what works and what doesn't before you dive in with both feet. The more prepared you are, the better the results that will come your way. Putting in a little hard work at the very beginning will help you go a long way in establishing a good line of passive income.

Any or all of these strategies are aimed at increasing traffic to your sites and increasing customer and visitor confidence in your content so that they are driven to clicking on an affiliate link on your site to complete the desired action that translates to affiliate earnings for you. It is important to remember that none of the above-mentioned strategies is a one-format-works-for-all type. You have to factor in what you have chosen to promote and who your target audience is and then make informed choices about the kind(s) of strategies to use.

Notwithstanding the above comment, an honest and upright website that gives correct information and recommendations without exaggeration is key to making a success of your affiliate program ventures. To reiterate, engaging, relevant, and updated content continues to hold sway over all other elements of a great website that attracts and retains loyal visitors.

Chapter 5: Top Affiliate Networks

While it is very difficult to come up with an exhaustive list of affiliate networks and programs for all of you hoping to make a beginning in this highly lucrative realm, this chapter deals with some of the top affiliate networks that have built a great reputation and brand for themselves. You can rest easy that the below-listed networks are above board and are backed by good products that you will be proud to promote on your website.

However, there could be smaller and equally upright networks that work well for you. What works well for you is dependent on many factors including what you plan to promote, who you would like to partner with, what niche is your website, and other such aspects. Please ensure that you have done ample homework on the advertisers and merchants that you choose to partner with before you sign on the dotted line.

Commission Junction – CJ, as it is referred to popularly, is a well-established trusted and consistent affiliate network that is a great company to partner with.

Rakuten Linkshare – This affiliate marketing service provider on advertiser service, large retailers as well as small merchants making its merchant base large enough to fit many affiliates comfortably.

ClickBank – A pioneer this field, ClickBank continues to have the support of smaller merchants and hence is attractive to many affiliates.

Amazon – Another pioneer in the field of affiliate marketing, Amazon has an extremely easy-to-use affiliate interface and has a humongous repertoire of products to choose from. These aspects make Amazon a very popular affiliate network and despite its lower-than-market affiliate payments, it is a great way to have a great head start for you to affiliate with this household name.

AvantLink – A comparatively new player in the market, AvantLink's many strategies are finding a lot of takers, which has made it to one of the top players in the realm of affiliate marketing.

ShareASale – Backed by a perception of integrity and honesty, ShareASale affiliate network has a lot of support from many affiliates across the world.

oneNetwork Direct – A great merchant for software products and services, oneNetwork Direct of Digital River, offers the best in the technological industry and has a presence all across the globe.

RevenueWire – RevenueWire is a specialist in technological products and has built a sterling reputation for ethical and sustainable commerce.

LinkConnector – This fairly large affiliate network offers products from a wide gambit of industries and merchants ranging from the Top 500 retailers on the internet to the smaller niches too.

Pepperjam – With a reputation for being very novice-friendly, Pepperjam affiliate network has a large fan-following both from merchants and super affiliates.

eBay Partner Network – Backed by QCP or Quality Click Pricing methodology for making affiliate payments, eBay Partner Network is a wonderful platform to partner with.

Affiliate Window – A hugely popular affiliate network in Britain with a slew of affiliate network awards under its belt, Affiliate Window is now making waves in the US too.

TradeDoubler – A pioneer of affiliate marketing in Europe, TradeDoubler was established in Sweden in 1999. It is still one of the most popular and a great performing affiliate network across all of Europe.

Avangate – Avangate is also an award-winning Europe-based affiliate network and specializes in SaaS and software products

Millionaire Network – Millionaire Network is open to affiliates on an invitation-only basis and focuses primarily on the success of the advertiser.

Zanox – Zanox is another of Europe's large affiliate network with a presence across the continent and an attractive payment scheme that makes it highly popular with affiliates.

WebGains – Backed by some old-fashioned yet robust value-system, this UK-based affiliate network is reputed to have an unshakable ethics-based reputation that is expected to enhance its longevity in the rather nebulous affiliate marketing field.

Adcommunal – This Canada-based affiliate network has grown from strength to strength and is one of the top players on the world stage of affiliate marketing.

PeerFly – A newcomer in the field of affiliate marketing, in a very short time, PeerFly has risen to one of the world's leading network backed by an excellently performing platform and a great team.

Since each site is unique and has its own weaknesses and strengths, it is impossible to come up with a complete list of available affiliate networks. The above list contains only the popular and most commonly used ones. The list highlights some of the large players across the world in the affiliate network realm and a few of them, I am sure, will work for you wonderfully, especially helping you through your steep learning curve.

As you gain more confidence and pick up more skills in the field, you will find more relevant, perhaps, more complex, yet better-paying merchants and advertisers that are in line with your own interests. You could at that time partner with these affiliates too as there are no regulations stopping you from any number of affiliates that you wish to partner with.

Picking the Right Affiliate Program

Now that we've gone into the list of reputed affiliate networks it's important to know how to choose an affiliate program that's good for you. All affiliate programs are different and you need to thoroughly inspect each one before you decide to jump into a deal. This section will cover the various things that you need to keep in my mind when you're finding the program that's the right fit for you.

Terms and Conditions

If you have decided on which company will be best for you and your customers, it's time to talk about terms. After all, that's what it's all about. The first thing to ask is how the program works. Are you paid purely for sales, or do you get a commission for leads? It is always better to argue for the latter as you will be tying up with someone who is considering you for your popularity. So it is best that you make full use of the opportunity and argue in your favor. It can make a big difference when it comes down to dollars, both in the amount you can expect to earn, and how long you will have to get paid.

How often do you get paid, and what is the minimum payout level? Many companies pay at the beginning or end of the month, or they may pay out twice a month – usually on the 15th and last day of the month. If you have a certain preference then you can consider asking them to change the time of payout. Check that the minimum payment threshold is not set too high. Obviously, it's not cost effective to pay out every time somebody clears $10, but if you have to rack up $100 or more before you see the color of your commission, it can be very de-motivating, unless you have a high conversion rate.

Finally, you need to know the rate of commission – both the bottom line and the structure. Some businesses operate a two-tier system, where you get paid for everyone who clicks through to your affiliate, and then receive a further commission if they complete a purchase. Other businesses just pay for one or the other. Commission rates for affiliates vary considerably from less than one percent for clicks to as much as 75% for some digital download products.

However, it's more realistic to work on a figure between 5% and 20%, and it's worth comparing similar companies to see if their commission rates and terms and conditions are similar.

Remember that money is important no doubt but you will also have to consider several other factors that will help you judge whether the products and services offered to comply with your standards. You cannot simply give anybody a nod and must lay down some ground rules for them. This might seem like a wrong thing to do but you need to maintain the standard of your blog and website as well. For this, you can send them a mail, listing the things that you will not be okay with on your blog or site such as sexually explicit content, weapons, adult products etc. There can be companies who will be looking for people that will be interested in letting out some space for such items. If they suspect that you have not explicitly mentioned these terms then they might start supplying you with links to such products. So it is important for you to try and check everything that they send across just to be cautious.

You must also discuss the rights and obligations and agree upon a termination clause. Remember, if you follow a path that is extremely professional, then it will be easy for you. You cannot take anything too lightly or casually, especially during the initial stages. Make sure you have everything signed and attested just to maintain an official record of your alliance and agreement. Once you are satisfied with everything and have made up your mind to go ahead with the deal then there should be nothing in your way to stop you.

Avoid paid-for programs

When you type 'Affiliate Marketing Programs' into Google, you will be inundated with hits. Some of these will be companies who ask you to pay to join their program. They will make use of fancy pamphlets that you can download and mention a well thought out payment plan. What's more, they will probably offer you a huge 'discount' to climb on board. The program's normal sign up cost is $99, but for today only, you will be admitted for the special price of just $20 – it may even be less than that. They will, in fact, make it look extremely attractive by canceling out the $99 with a big red cross and write $20 only next to it. All you have to do now is close the window and move away from such programs.

It goes without saying that there are a million suspicious websites out there all of whom promise you something but do something else. Now, while I am not saying that these people might cheat you, even if they are to charge you a high amount of money it will be for their profit and they will not be bothered about you or your website. So don't trust these and only trust your instincts in doing the right thing.

As has already been noted, the affiliate business doesn't pay any commission to you until they make a sale and remember this is a sale they wouldn't ace without your help. So why would they want you to pay for the privilege of widening their retail reach? It was mentioned before that nobody would be willing to part with their money just to promote someone else. That's like saying Microsoft wants to hire you but you need to pay them fees for it.

It can sometimes feel like the right choice to make, especially if the website you visited is promising you many things. I am sure you have also considered it many times just to get started with affiliate marketing at the earliest. You have to be more patient when it comes to affiliate marketing because, otherwise, you might end up getting scammed.

But who in their right senses would use their credit card details or check into their online banking account to transfer money to a suspicious source? Not only is it dangerous for your account but what if you end up having an identity theft?

So, as a rule of thumb, don't trust any website on affiliate marketing that promises you good business if you pay them some money first. That is not how it works and you will have to find a different way in order for you to establish a proper affiliate marketing set up.

Remember, if you stay too long on a website you will be tempted to check it out in detail. Instead, choose to exit as soon as possible and also clear your cookies.

Another thing that seems to happen is that companies charge affiliates to join deals in high-ticket items. You may make a tasty profit from each conversion, but realistically are the people who will be visiting your site going to be interested in high-ticket stuff, even if it is linked to your niche? Even if you can answer 'yes' to that one, you're a beginner in the affiliate marketing game. Isn't it better to make your mistakes for free?

Check the Business

We've established that any affiliate you pair with should complement and add value to your site for your visitors, as well as return an income for you. We read on how it is possible for you to increase the number of customers that visit the affiliates page and how much more business both of you can establish together if you understand each other well.

But in order for this to happen, you must initiate the process of looking for the best affiliates to tie up with. So make sure that you do some research and try and choose the best one. After all, you have the choice to nod or refuse a certain client depending on whether or not you like them.

One way to look for the good ones is by checking out what other blogs like yours are hosting. You can randomly check the websites that other bloggers like you are hosting, especially the popular ones. Once you have a few, you can decide to contact them yourself and show them your blog or website. After you get a reply, you can skim through all the important ones.

Maybe you've looked at a few business websites and are wondering who to approach. You can decide to shortlist 5 or 6 of them and go to the next step.

The first thing to do is check out the website for navigation. Is it easy to find the products your visitors will be interested in, and how easy is it to complete the purchase once the affiliate link takes the reader to the product?

This is important because you have to believe in the website yourself before you decide to host them for others. You will have to place yourself in the shoes of others just so that you have a chance to look at your blog from a third party perspective. For this, you must understand how the affiliate website operates.

One way to check this out is to place an order on the site yourself, so you can check out the purchase process on behalf of your visitors. Is the navigation process straightforward, from adding the item to your virtual basket? Is it possible for you to edit the items present in your cart? Can you increase or decrease the volume of the products easily? Does it have an option to add in a coupon code? Is it possible to redeem any points? What about the payment process? Does the site support PayPal?

Many online purchasers are wary about using credit cards online and prefer the speed, simplicity, and security of paying via PayPal. And it's worth returning an item so that you can check out their standards of customer service. By placing affiliate links on your site, you are effectively endorsing the company and its products to your followers, so you need to know they will get good service.

Imagine what would happen if you start putting links to websites that are slightly tough to navigate or the buying process is complicated? People won't be interested in clicking on the links and the company might not garner as many hits as is necessary.

Once you've checked out that side of the business, and are completely satisfied with what you have, it's time to speak to someone about becoming an affiliate, so that any queries you have can be addressed before you commit yourself.

Make sure you have everything sorted out and jot down the questions in terms of importance and priority. Once sorted, start asking them one by one if it is a telephone chat or you can also shoot them a mail with all your queries. Remember, it is never a bad idea to be well informed about something. After all, you are hosting their website and it is best that they give answers to everything that you wish to know. It might take them some time to get back to you and you can give them a couple of days' time to go through all your questions and answer them one by one.

If nobody is available for you, or they keep you waiting for several days for a reply, maybe you should move on. After all, if they can't make the effort to answer your queries before you become a partner, it isn't likely that they will do so once you've joined the program. So don't keep waiting on someone who is not keen on replying to you even if they say things like "sorry for the delay, we regret it."

Chapter 6: Affiliate Marketing Via Social Media Networks

Affiliate marketing via the various social media networks is, perhaps, the most fun way, and of course, a great way to enhance earnings. Working as an affiliate allows you to straight away start earning money without the hassles associating with creating, packaging, and advertising a product on your own.

Affiliate marketing via the social media allows you to leverage on the goodwill of your friends, family, and followers to get plenty of traffic and sales which in turn will get you good money. This chapter gives you some insight on how to use your social media platforms to increase affiliate income.

Create a redirect link for the affiliate – Instead of embedding a raw link (that very few people will be interesting in clicking) on your FB page, create and insert a redirect link that will take the visitor to the advertiser's site.

Quality content – As in the case of your blog, here too, create quality content first. This will attract more visitors to your page and the increased traffic can then be rerouted to affiliate links. A compelling story fitted with a link at the end is a sure shot winner. The content you create could take any form: a blog post, an FB post, YouTube video, a Podcast, and more.

Ensure you have images of the product(s) that you are promoting – A visual treat is always better remembered and retained by the human brain than mere text even if the text is highly compelling. Ensure you have a picture or a link to the picture of the product to enhance chances of the sale closing successfully.

Create and grow you email list from your social media connections – One critical aspect to note here is that social media sites themselves work as affiliates and hence if you aggressively use that platform to grow your affiliate income, you could be banned. While keeping this in mind, you could create and grow an email list from your social media contacts and connections and then send your affiliate links through email. This will help you mitigate the "banning" risk while giving you headway into genuinely interested buyers of the products and services you are promoting.

Promote only genuine and good-quality offers – Be wary of fraud and cheap offers and promote the really good ones only. This attitude makes you and your social connections happy; you will be happy that you are getting paid well by way of healthy commissions and your friends will be happy that they have access to a great deal.

Leverage the power of autoresponder emails – Autoresponder tools such as Aweber are powerful inventions that are extremely handy for affiliates. You could set the responder to send 7 emails (one every day for the first 7 days) after a new person connects with you. These emails can be any value-addition mails such as e-courses and study materials that are relevant for the subscriber. This value-addition offering will make the person your fan for life and he or she will be more inclined to click on affiliate links that you send to them or cmbed on your social media page.

The above strategies are great ways to increase your fan base on social media and then leverage that large base to generate sales and leads under your affiliate marketing program. Social media reaches every nook and corner of the world and it would be foolhardy not to take advantage of this huge reach and dig into untapped business opportunities.

Chapter 7: Affiliate Marketing Scams

As a novice in the highly challenging field of affiliate marketing, it is extremely important for you not to fall for scams and fraudulent networks and advertisers. The field of affiliate marketing per se is very legitimate but like any other industry, it is prone to misuse by mischief mongers and scamsters looking for a quick buck. Here are some of the common scams that you are bound to come across as you learn the ropes of the affiliate marketing.

Fraudulent Training Programs – Like all newbies in any field, wanting to attend a course is a common thing you would like to do before you plunge into the game. There will be hundreds of entities promising you the world and telling you that they have a magic wand to make you rich overnight with affiliate marketing.

Do not fall for such cheap gimmicks. Most likely, they are people waiting to make a fast buck by giving you material that has little or no real substance. You will merely lose out on the fees that you paid to join the course. Check, find out more, ask people who have done the course before, and only then make the fee payment and complete the training.

Get Rich Overnight Offers – There are hundreds of fraudulent mails floating around that promise you anything between $2000 and $10000 within a week by working for just 2-3 hours a day. Again, beware of such marketing gimmicks. You know it cannot be true. If it was true, there would be a huge line of aspirants and this kind of project (if true) would never need a marketing strategy. It would sell by itself. On the contrary, such "too good to be true" scenarios would ideally be kept secret.

There is no such thing in a legitimate affiliate marketing program. It entails all the hard work and diligence already spelt out in this book and nothing less to make a success of the program and make a decent amount of money regularly.

No Service or Product to sell – These offers are completely fraudulently. If someone is willing to shell out money without wanting anything in return, you should know that it is a straightforward fraud. These seeming "business opportunities" are structured like a pyramid where money is simply passed on and there is no one actually making any money. You will not only lose your investment but also please know that such schemes are totally illegal.

Programs that need you to make an initial payment – All legitimate affiliate programs are completely free. If someone is asking for initial payment, then your antennae should go up and you should totally avoid that person and/or email.

Scams based on Domain names – Here too there are multiple emails floating around that tell you the following story: The fraudsters can see from some unnamed or fancily named records that xyz.com is registered in your name and someone else in the country of origin of this scam (usually China) wants to register his or her domain name as xyz.cn. To protect your business interests, they will want you to send some money and then all payments in relation to xyz.cn will also start flowing to you!

This is utter rubbish; do not fall for it. If you send that initial payment, you can say goodbye to it forever, because if you notice you never owned the domain name xyz.com at all!!

Avoid all these kinds of scams by doing due diligence. Ask around, ask Google, look up the company website that is selling you these programs, and finally if it is too good to be true and then it is definitely not true. Do not fall for it and stay away!

Remember as long as there are people to fool, mock at and cheat, there will be people fooling, mocking and making a quick buck by cheating! Do not be one of those who fall for these kinds of "easy" money fast and without thinking.

Chapter 8: Affiliate Marketing without a Website

One of the most common ways in which you can launch yourself into the world of affiliate marketing is by creating a website. And if you are in it for the long haul, then it will be in the best interest of your business that you create a website.

However, if you are still at the stage of learning about web designing or if you are amongst those who are not interested in creating a website, but still want to be a part of affiliate marketing, then fret not because there is an easy solution to this problem. And in this chapter, you will learn about the various ways in which you can get started with affiliate marketing without the use of a website.

Remember that the main objective of affiliate marketing is to provide you with a way in which you can put up your affiliate link in front of the target audience. As mentioned earlier, building a website is the most common approach adopted. But then again, the path you opt for is entirely up to you. With this basic objective in mind, let us look at various methods that you can use for getting your affiliate link to the target audience.

Ads and Reviews

You can use classified sites to promote your affiliate product. You must already be familiar with websites like Craigslist, eBay and so on to look for any product you want. The same can be used to promote your affiliate product too. You can write ads or even reviews about your affiliate products and then post them along with the affiliate link.

Viral Marketing

Viral marketing means spreading awareness about something very quickly. So, for doing this, you will need to figure out a product that can go viral online. A viral product is a product that has been created with the specific intention to spread it quickly to a large number of people. This is one of the fastest ways in which you can gain attention for your product.

What you can do perhaps is write a very short eBook, preferably less than 30 pages or even a report on a particular topic that interests you, and then insert the links to your affiliate products in it. Then you can distribute it to the audience using whichever means you have in mind. You could sell it, put it up on other websites or even just casually inform people that they can buy it. For starters, you can start selling this eBook on eBay for a nominal price. Ensure that whatever you are writing about is actually informational and useful. No one would want to go through a document filled with affiliate links.

Pay per Click (PPC)

This is not a method that would come as recommended. In this method, you will have to create a lot of pay per click or PPC campaigns making use of search engines like Google, Yahoo, Bing, etc. and then you will have to promote the merchant website by making use of your affiliate link. So, this is not a straightforward method because instead of directly making use of PPC to promote your own affiliate link, you will send all this to your merchant.

There are two things that you will need to know about before selecting this option. It might just happen that the merchant website might not accept your affiliate link. You will have to compete with other advertisers for the space available. And you might as well forget about your ad if it isn't well written and it is not attractive and not just this but you will even have to bid an amount higher than the rest. And the second aspect is that you will have no quality control over the merchant's page. If the merchant website does not have proper content or it is of poor quality, then you would probably end up paying a larger sum than necessary.

Blogs and Forums

All you have to do is zero in on a product that interests you and you are keen on promoting, then start marketing this product by posting about it on various forums and blogs. The question is how do you direct the users to your affiliate link? Well, the answer is quite simple because all you have to do is make use of your affiliate link as your signature. If you make yourself an active member on any forum and if you have followers, then this will just be an added advantage. But then again, you should be cautious about the kind of blogs and forums you decide to post about your products on. You need to post on such blogs and forums that deal with a topic complimentary to your own product or at least along similar lines to what you are promoting. If you want to market a fashion affiliated product, then you might not find any enthusiastic supporters on a forum meant for car parts.

Along the same line of thought, if you are really interested in making a big splash on any public forum, then you will need to be careful about the content you are posting. Ensure that the content is not only interesting but helpful too. Try becoming an active member of the forum. And once you have managed to establish yourself and garnered the attention of others, then a greater number of users will want to visit your link. And also remember to maintain some etiquette while posting online.

Don't spam the blog or forum with unnecessary posts, as this might eventually lead to you being banned from the forum or your posts might be deleted.

YouTube

YouTube is one of the most popular ways in which you can get your message across to literally millions of users within no time. YouTube has nearly a billion visitors every month. That is simply incredible and you could very well use it to your advantage. All you need is a webcam, an innovative idea and the internet. These three things are more than enough to start your own channel on YouTube. You can insert your affiliate links in the description of your channel and even in your videos. In this manner, you will be able to convert your followers into affiliate users and this will generate profits for you.

Select a niche you are interested in, and once you have decided that, then you can start a video series about it and you can insert your affiliate links into it. The viewers would already be interested in the video series created by you and, for this reason, it is likely that they would even be curious about the affiliate product you are promoting.

There are two rules and you should abide by them if you want to use this method successfully. The first rule is that the content you are posting should provide the viewers with some value and monetary gain for you should be a secondary objective. If you start the series with only the monetary aspect in your mind and want to make money from your link, then this behavior will get you listed as spam and all the hard work you put into this will be useless. If what you have produced is meaningful and interesting, then the chances of gaining attention and even respect of likely users will increase. The second rule is that you don't create something that is misleading. You would be violating YouTube's policies if the video you have posted is unrelated to the link or even if the title or description is misleading. This is something that you would want to avoid.

Video marketing on YouTube is easy, but then, if you aren't careful, it can be quite risky. It is highly likely that the affiliate links can be branded as spam. So the best way to avoid this is by being honest and being useful. Ensure that you have quality controls in place and the content is meaningful. Don't indulge in any behavior that can be listed as spam. If you are interested in nutrition then you could have instructional videos related to cooking or you could even have discussions related to this topic. Anything that might prove to be useful for the viewers is the best way to gain attention.

There are some precautions you can take to ensure that your videos aren't listed as spam. The first thing you can do is to not include too many affiliate links in your video. It is better to include one link in your description and another one in the video, provided it is relevant. The second thing you can do is to mention that the link is an affiliate link or that you are an affiliate. You can also contact YouTube to ensure that you aren't in any trouble. If you have managed to acquire a valuable viewership then this means that the chance of making money from your affiliate links will increased.

Hub

A Hub is like a miniature of a website, it is just a page. So, on this page, you can talk about anything that you are interested in. You can base your content on the affiliate market and related products you are interested in.

Your Hub would be put up on the HubPages site and it is perfectly alright even if you don't have any knowledge about web designing. You can still make it look decent and professional. The advantage of making use of Hub is that you don't have to code the page in HTML. You can create the page on any topic you are interested in. You can insert various ads, reviews or any other content that you want.

Another good feature of this is that it is even a social networking platform. Even being simply present on HubPages you can attract traffic towards the topics you are interested in.

Conclusion

Affiliate marketing is here to stay and with an intention to be a stakeholder in this rather interesting and lucrative field you should endeavor to pick up the right skills, know the correct information, and understand how to implement your learning prudently before you plunge in.

It is a great career opportunity for those who have managed to break the code and have made sustained and persistent efforts without being demoralized by initial setbacks. Making an entry into this challenging environment, getting that first small break, coding and decoding large amounts of data and information to leverage to your advantage, and most importantly a willingness to learn from your failures; all these require lots of hard work, diligence, and commitment from your side.

Yes, it is a huge challenge to overcome; but once done, the opportunities are unlimited for you. Heartened by this knowledge, I hope you pick up this chance to enhance your earnings.

And finally, do not fall for scamsters and cheats. Think before you leap; use common sense and avoid things that do not make sense. There are hundreds of legitimate ways of making money vide affiliate marketing. Although the process of setting up and maintenance may seem tough, it is quite possible to make a success of your venture.

There are many people making great amounts of money. Follow them; be motivated by them, and find the courage to start off. In fact, I believe, that affiliate marketing business opportunities if leveraged well can be a legacy to leave behind for your future generation.

Thank you again for purchasing this book!

I hope this book was able to help you to start off on the exciting and lucrative journey of affiliate marketing. The next step for you is to start implementing your learning and set up actionable tasks which should be reviewed regularly to see if you are going down the right path.

www.ingramcontent.com/pod-product-compliance
Lightning Source LLC
Chambersburg PA
CBHW071651210326
41597CB00017B/2181